LOCAL
SCHOOLS

The Nearby History Series

David E. Kyvig, *Series Editor*
Myron A. Marty, *Consulting Editor*

Local Schools

Exploring Their History

Ronald E. Butchart

The American Association for State and Local History
Nashville, Tennessee

Library of Congress Cataloging in Publication Data

Butchart, Ronald E.
  Local Schools

  (The Nearby history series)
  Bibliography: p. 101
  Includes Index.
  1. Public schools—United States—Historiography.
2. Community and school—United States—Historiography.
I. Title. II. Series
LA9.B87   1986   371'.01'0973   86-22276
ISBN O-910050-82-1

Cover design by Gillian Murrey

Contents

Editors' Introduction

COMMUNITIES WITHOUT UNDERSTANDINGS OF THEIR PASTS resemble people suffering from amnesia, unable to remember from where they came, how they responded to needs or challenges, from whence they drew affection and support or opposition, and where they intended to go. History, the contemplation and evaluation of the past, serves society much as memory serves the individual in identifying circumstances, providing a guide to satisfactory behavior, and offering a standard of comparison across time and situation. In this sense, history is far more than a remembrance of things past, though it certainly includes that. History represents a means of coming to terms with the past, of developing an awareness of previous influences, current conditions, and future possibilities. Just as memory helps the individual avoid repeating the same discoveries, behaviors, and mistakes, historical knowledge helps the community avoid starting at the beginning each time it addresses an issue.

History, in addition to being useful, is accessible. Any literate person can master and pursue most historical research techniques and can understand and critically evaluate historical explanations as well. Futhermore, history is interesting. Whether reading other people's mail, understanding how ordinary people lived their everyday lives at other times and in other places, or assessing how institutions rose or decayed, the individual studying history constantly finds exciting opportunities to learn about the human condition.

All of these values of history hold as true for the nearby world as for the larger sphere. English historian H.P.R. Finberg considered "the family, the local community, the national state, and the supra-national society as a series of concentric circles." He observed, "Each requires to be studied with constant reference to the one outside it; but the inner rings are not the less perfect circles for being wholly surrounded and enclosed by the outer." In fact, understanding the history of the world close at hand is of great value, for it is this history that shapes the circumstances we must deal with directly and constantly.

In 1982 we wrote a book professing the importance of taking a look at the history of the close-at-hand world and attempting to provide assistance in so doing. *Nearby History: Exploring the Past around You*, published by AASLH, was by design merely an introduction to a broad and complex topic. The book sought to raise questions for consideration, to point out the sorts of materials that exist for historical research, to suggest generally how they may be used, and to indicate some of the published works that may offer useful models or comparisons in nearby historical topics. *Nearby History* was predicated on the belief that useful inquiry into the nearby past was not an undertaking for academic professionals alone, but could be pursured in a worthwhile fashion by any interested student or out-of-school adult. We intended to stir interest and to indicate how local concerns could comfortably mesh with sophisticated historical thinking.

Growing interest in the subjects and objectives addressed in *Nearby History* persuaded us that a need exists for a series of books focused on specific aspects of the close-at-hand world. Particular issues and institutions in the community deserving historical consideration pose individual problems of research and analysis. Schools, churches, homes, businesses, and public places of the nearby world should be addressed historically, each in its own way. The volumes in the "Nearby History" series will give outstanding specialists in these areas the opportunity to offer guidance and insight to readers engaged in their own local investigations.

Ronald E. Butchart's *Local Schools: Exploring Their History* is the inaugural volume in the "Nearby History" series. It asks stimulating questions about the role of education as well as about the nature of schools within a community. It identifies sources of information and means by which such materials can lead to insight. Butchart's own research has ranged over eastern, southern, midwestern, and far western American schools, from post-Civil War Reconstruction to the recent past. He draws on this rich and varied body of significant work to offer a host of worthwhile suggestions for historical inquiry. *Local Schools* calls attention to the possibilities of meaningful investigation of the history of education within the community.

We wish to acknowledge our appreciation to Betty Doak Elder of the University of Alabama at Birmingham and former director of the AASLH Press for her encouragement in the development of this series. We would also like to thank Charles M. Dye of the College of Education and George W. Knepper of the Department of History at the University of Akron for their helpful readings of this manuscript.

DAVID E. KYVIG, Series Editor
MYRON A. MARTY, Consulting Editor

Acknowledgements

SEVERAL PEOPLE AND ORGANIZATIONS CONTRIBUTED TIME, ideas, and skills in the course of my work on this book. Without them it would not have been written. A special word of acknowledgement and gratitude to David E. Kyvig and Myron A. Marty, patient and persistent editors, who conceived of the series of which this volume is a part. Gary Barnes gave me sound advice on photography, lent me his camera, and worked darkroom magic to improve marginal negatives. Fellow historians Nancy Green, Dick Altenbaugh, Jeff Mirel, Tracey Mitrano, Platt Cline, and Lisa Fine responded enthusiastically to my project and offered insightful contributions, which I have scattered about in the text. Thanks, friends.

I am constantly delighted with the helpfulness and friendliness of the overworked and undervalued staff at local and county historical societies around the country. Arlene Busse of the Sibley County Historical Society in Minnesota deserves particular thanks for her extensive correspondence with a total stranger and for her remarkable assistance when I visited Gaylord, Minnesota. People like her add a measure of grace to the world and a measure of joy to the work of historians. My thanks as well to the two dozen other historical societies and related institutions I visited.

RONALD E. BUTCHART

Illustrations

THE AUTHOR AND PUBLISHER GRATEFULLY ACKNOWLÉDGE the following individuals and organizations for granting permission to reproduce, on the pages listed below, pictorial materials from their collections.

Cortland County, New York, Historical Society, pp. 7, 52, 53, 64
David E. Kyvig, p. 23
National Archives and Records Administration, cover, p. 107
Eugene and Asterie Provenzo, pp. 16, 19, 29, 104, 112, 113
Renville County, Minnesota, Historical Society, pp. 62, 63
Sibley County Courthouse, Gaylord, Minnesota, pp. 38, 39, 57
Stevens County, Minnesota, Historical Society, p. 83
All other photographs are from the author's personal collection.

Local Schools

·1·

The History of Nearby Education

THIS BOOK IS DESIGNED TO ASSIST ANYONE WHO IS preparing to explore the history of his or her local schools. Whether a local history novice casting about for a topic or an experienced local historian turning to nearby education, a student meeting a history assignment or a citizen desiring insight into the community's schools, you will find in these pages guidance, suggestions, and access to tools and material. The book will encourage the less experienced to dive into an exciting avocation. Veteran local historians will, I trust, find new approaches and be challenged to expand their skills.

We will turn our attention momentarily to the sorts of topics one may approach when exploring the local history of education. There are many more issues than usually occur to the casual observer. We will then examine some of the specific questions one may pose, a process that helps focus the research. Once the plans, in the form of a specific research agenda, have been developed, we will discuss the available strategies—the sources of historical data and the many ways to extract meaning from that data. We will consider problems of analysis, evaluation, interpretation, and presentation and close with a selective overview of professional histories of local education—histories that serve as models or provide hypotheses to test.

Before tackling those issues, however, there are some considerations about history that require at least brief comment, for they are basic assumptions throughout this book. We will conclude this chapter with some specific reasons for pursuing the history of local schools and some of the topics to select.

It may be well, here, to define more precisely what history is, for many people go around with inaccurate notions of history in their heads. For many Americans, history is merely the literary form of the museum or antique

1

What might have led the patrons of this school to have gone to the extra expense and trouble of building an octagonal schoolhouse? Where may the historian of nearby education look to find clues to its construction and meaning? What may the building itself add to a history of education in its neighborhood?

shop. History, in this view, simply shows things as they were, just as the museum's display of carriages or quaint clothing or obsolete tools shows concretely how people once traveled, dressed, or worked. The historian's job, then, is to tell the story with as much photographic clarity as possible.

That view is one that James Davidson and Mark Lytle call the "everyday view of history." They point out that history is not so simple. The way things were depends on point of view, available evidence, and interpretation. History is, they assert, "the act of selecting, analyzing, and writing about the past. It is something that is done, that is constructed, rather than an inert body of data that lies scattered through the archives."

History is, roughly speaking, a form of collective memory. Both history and our personal memories rely inevitably on interpretation. Memory, like history, "is something that is done, something that is constructed."

Think first about memory. Memory is not a precise replica of an event or place; instead it is a particular reconstruction of the event or place. What we remember depends on what was important to us in the situation. My memory of high school, for instance, doubtlessly differs from my classmates' and probably departs radically from the memories my teachers have of those same years. Probably few of the teachers have a clear memory of me. They may recall, however, the way our classrooms were arranged and the difficult time they had engaging our attention to learn Spanish vocabulary, the periodic table, or the meaning of Manifest Destiny.

My classmates and I, on the other hand, recall few of the hours we spent in classrooms and study halls. But ask us about the cars we drove, the sports we played, the dates we had, or the pictures we hung in our lockers, and we display vivid memories. We do not all remember the same things by any means, but we would have many parallel memories. We selected very differently than our mentors, however, when we packed our mental baggage and moved on into adult life.

That is not all there is to say about memory, of course. My memory can be altered with new knowledge. I have no recollection whatsoever of an English class my junior year, yet one of my teachers could show me in my records that I not only took such a class but received a passing grade in it. While that evidence might not cause me to recall the teacher, the classroom, or the curriculum, I would nonetheless now know that I indeed took such a course. Similarly, were I to go to a class reunion, my classmates and I would doubtlessly restore to memory events and faces that we had long since mislaid.

Thus, memory is selective and susceptible to modification and extension. So it is with the minutiae of history. Through historical research, we find evidence that modifies and extends our knowledge, and we select from the vast quantity of available data those facts that seem to be the most important.

But we do not stop with the facts, either when we are remembering or when we are doing history. It is impossible to tell a story "as it was." We will always interpret as well. Even if my high school teachers and my class-mates were able to modify each others' memories so that we remembered the same things, we would still, in all likelihood, differ in our interpreta-tion of the events. My teachers' interpretation would spring from their con-viction that education has intellectual and moral purposes above all. They would recount those years in terms of the classroom work, the books we studied, the ideas we considered, and the colleges we entered after their classes. The former students would tell a tale centering on our social life in the halls, the auditorium, the gymnasium, and the parking lot. We might recall the classroom, too, but the focus would be on the crush every male student had on Mrs. Six, what a creep our social studies teacher was, and our strategies for getting Mr. Paul to talk about anything other than geome-try. Our interpretations would create very different stories.

As we construct history, we are involved in much the same process. We seek to extend our knowledge of the facts as far as possible but, in the process, select only those facts that appear important. We might, for example, have access to information on the location of all the drinking fountains in a public school building in the 1940s, or the names of the night janitorial staff in 1956, or the number of tons of coal used to heat the building annually, but we might not use that information in any history we choose to write. We analyze evidence to attempt to understand its significance; for example, we might examine whether the declining rates of electoral participation in school elections indicated apathy, dissatisfaction with the choices availa-ble, or approval of the general patterns of school board decisions. Our interpre-tation affects our selection and analysis. But if we are careful, reflective historians, evidence and honest analysis guide our interpretation.

Studying Local—or Nearby—History

Traditionally, historians refer to the history of a town or county as *local* or *community history*. Research into the physical aspects of the human-created past—a factory, a public building, or locomotive headlights—is called *material culture studies* or, occasionally, *industrial archaeology*. *Family history*, obviously, is that branch of social history that concerns itself with domestic arrangements. David E. Kyvig and Myron A. Marty suggest that the separation of the history of nearby phenomena is artificial and does not reflect what historians usually do. Kyvig and Marty suggest a new name for the endeavor—"nearby history." In discussing ways to pursue the history of local educational institutions and to use the techniques of community studies, material culture study, and family history, I will follow Kyvig and Marty's suggestion and refer to these efforts primarily as the history of nearby education.

Why pursue nearby history? The most obvious answer is that it is most convenient for us. The sources are close at hand, and they may be simple to find and easy to gain permission for use. To write the history of the United States's intervention in the Russian Revolution requires access to the American and Soviet national archives, an inconvenience for all but the most well-funded professional historian.

Just as important, nearby history begins with subjects with which we are already familiar to some extent, or in which we have some immediate, almost intrinsic interest. Few people know that American soldiers occupied portions of Russian soil in 1918. Not many can sustain much interest in the topic; it is too distant in many ways. But to turn our attention to the ways local farm wives lived their daily lives at the turn of the century, to styles of public architecture, or to a village's most notable crime is to develop insight into events that touch our own lives more directly and allow us more fully to see ourselves as part of a historical stream.

Furthermore, studying nearby history is the most natural and logical way for us to understand the broader historical currents of our society and our world. Kyvig and Marty provide an illustration that is worth repeating in this regard. The world, they write (borrowing from H.P.R. Finberg, an English historian), may be conceived of as a series of concentric circles. We are at the center, surrounded by our family. Beyond the family lies the circle of the community; beyond it, the nation; surrounding all, the international community. Events in one circle affect events in the other circles. For example, international peace obviously affects the nation in myriad ways. Both peace and its effects on the nation directly affect the community and families. Similarly, a national recession affects the international economy, as well as the financial health of local communities and of families. While the effects are not as profound as we work from the center of the circle outward, surely the cumulative effects of family decisions eventually alter the structures of communities and of nations. That happened in the nineteenth century when the size of the average family dropped dramatically and again in the last century as families progressively abandoned subsistent and self-sufficient lives for reliance on the marketplace.

Why Education's Nearby History?

Let me suggest some strictly practical reasons first. Chief among them is the fact that there are more sources readily available in the area of the nearby history of education than there are for just about any other nearby institution to which we may turn our attention. It may just be, in fact, that there is also a greater *variety* of sources as well, as we shall see when we examine the types and locations of sources to use. Public education, for instance, is at least a century old in all but the very newest communities in the country, and in much of the nation, it is a great deal older than that. Few institutions have been subjected to more record-keeping. It is fitting, perhaps, that the institution that taught most people to record through writing should have extensive records itself on all aspects of its operation. While private schools, higher education, and other forms of formal education may have existed for longer or shorter periods of time than the public sector, they, too, have kept voluminous records or have been monitored by various state and private agencies whose papers are available. Thus, education's nearby history is worth pursuing just in terms of the availability of solid historical evidence.

Another practical consideration is the fact that nearly everyone has had experience in the formal educational institutions of our society. While even our literate forebears of just a century ago might have had only four or five years of rather irregular schooling, most Americans today have been in schools for no less than twelve years, and a remarkable number have sixteen or more years of schooling. Thus, by pursuing the nearby history of education, we are not at the disadvantage of trying to do the history of something that is foreign. Just as important, our audience will almost assuredly share that background and will draw on its own experience as it considers the history we present.

There are also intellectual reasons to study education's nearby history. The most important reason for attention to the history of education, nearby or more distant, is that the historical mode of inquiry can answer a number of important questions about this ubiquitous process. Without a historical perspective, the public finds itself constantly "reinventing the wheel" when it comes to the ways in which schools train the next generation. We will talk at length in the next chapter about the sorts of questions that may be explored through the history of nearby schooling. Let me simply suggest here one or two of the more intriguing issues.

Ultimately, the central question is this: Why does a society educate in the ways it does? Or more simply: Why schools? Whether we examine how children were educated in another era, the content of social studies text-books used in the schools in the 1930s, or the quality of the experience of being a teacher, we are posing, in one way or another, an age-old philosophical question: What do schools do? The answer is not as straight-forward as it appears, but it is of utmost significance, for the community's answer to that question determines much about the shape and quality of the educational experience. As we pursue that question, we begin to glimpse the ways in which formal education is embedded in a social and cultural context and to see the constraints placed on it.

Students in the past would not recognize the grading system found in most modern schools. The assign-ment of letter or number grades and the calculation of grade point averages are of relatively recent origin. When did letter or number grading begin in the educational institutions near you? What sorts of grading preceded it? Would a different mode of assessment alter students' perception of schooling? Pictured above are "merit awards," which teachers in some nineteenth-century schools presented to students as a form of academic recognition.

Connected to that, and serving as another reason for the study of education's nearby history, is the issue of policy decisions. Perhaps you are a member of the local school board or an interested citizen. You face difficult choices that must be guided by an intelligent understanding of the issues. What direction should the district go? Should there be more emphasis on vocational training or athletics? At the expense of what? Should more attention be given to the gifted? At the expense of whom? With what consequences? What happened in the past when these sorts of questions were posed? How have we historically answered the question, why schools? Are we comfortable with those answers? What is the relationship among those answers, our reaction to those answers, and the issues we face today? What other purposes for schooling might we entertain? What are the implications of adopting a different educational mission? Using the history of our schools and colleges to illuminate contemporary policy questions may not make our choices easier (it may, in fact, illuminate how problematical the whole endeavor is), but it will doubtlessly make the process of reaching decisions more reflective and intelligent.

Topics for Education's Nearby History

The topics to work on are limited only by the sources available and your own imagination. Local public schools may be the first institutions to come to mind, but you certainly need not limit yourself to them. Private and parochial schools are excellent candidates for careful study. You may focus on an individual school—Franklin Pierce Elementary School or P.S. 94—on the public schools of an entire community or district, or on all the educational opportunities for children within a village or city. You may limit your research chronologically or take in the entire period in which the target school or schools existed. You would not be violating the notion of nearby history by expanding your vision to an entire county or diocese. And you may expand your vision vertically if you wish, taking in the sweep of formal education from preschool through the local college or university.

Nor are you limited to the education of children. Nearby education includes the history of academies or colleges, trade schools and business schools (largely ignored by researchers), and adult evening courses in local schools. You may reach even farther afield to study the educational roles of local libraries, literary and debating societies—popular in the nineteenth century especially—women's clubs, and so forth.

You may prefer an approach that is less institutional in focus. For instance, much of value can be learned by looking at the education of women, blacks, Hispanics, immigrants, working-class children, the handicapped, or any other discrete population within nearby educational institutions. Or you may be concerned with teachers, parent-teacher groups, administrators, school boards, or the local political coalitions that organized around educational issues. We still know far too little about students themselves—their organizations, student life, student perceptions of the educational process, and the ways schools came to organize students' leisure time.

Other approaches suggest themselves depending on your particular interests. If you are interested in the history of ideas, examinations of changing public perceptions of the purposes of education in your community, or curricular innovations, or the view of the schools implicit in the actions of the school board or the statements of superintendents and other administrators would make challenging projects. If your forte is economics, consider a history of school financing in your school district or city. Or relate the nearby history of schools to the various concerns of social history. What, for instance, was the impact of the Depression or of wartime on nearby schools?

For those who have little experience with historical research, a closing word. You may easily become intimidated by the prospect of plunging into a field with no more expertise than you now have. The range of methodologies available to the historian has been growing every decade. How can you possibly expect to do a competent job with no experience? There is too much to know.

There is no need to be intimidated. You need not know all the methods or even most of them. The work of the historian has more in common with old craft traditions than with modern professions. In a craft—carpentry, for example—you need not have all of the knowledge and tools of the master craftsman in order to do a careful, commendable job of adding a room, building a table, or remodeling a bathroom. A few basic tools and a book to give you hints will not make you an expert, but they can give you confidence and guidance. As you master those tools and perfect a few skills, you can try new tools and skills. This book introduces many. Try those that have some promise for you, but do not feel that you have to be competent in all of them to do good history. Native intelligence, careful work, and a willingness to learn are the only serious prerequisites.

Suggested Readings

The indispensable handbook for nearby history is David E. Kyvig and Myron A. Marty, *Nearby History: Exploring the Past around You* (Nashville: American Association for State and Local History, 1982). I have quoted in this chapter from pages 4 and 7 of that volume.

For an entertaining, insightful, and helpful discussion on the work of historians, you can hardly do better than James West Davidson and Mark Hamilton Lytle, *After the Fact: The Art of Historical Detection* (New York: Alfred A. Knopf, 1983). The quotations are from their prologue, pages xiii and xvii.

·2·

Defining Topics and Focus

BEFORE A CARPENTER BEGINS THE ACTUAL CONSTRUCTION of a building, he must have a clear sense of what he wants to build. He must have plans, either in his head or, preferably, on paper. As historians we too must have plans, though they need not be as detailed, and we can frequently change our plans as we go along. But without plans, without a clear sense of what we want to know and the ways we intend to discover it, our effort to construct a history of nearby education is likely to end up as haphazard and ill-conceived as a house built by a carpenter with no plans.

The carpenter plans by deciding first on the type of building he wants—is it to be an office, a barn, a house? Then he determines the size of the structure, its style of construction, and the materials to be used. Finally, he draws his blueprints, noting exact sizes of rooms, locations of closets, wiring, plumbing, windows, doors, and so forth. Only then is he ready to survey the site and break the ground.

If our efforts in researching history are roughly analogous to the work of other craftspeople, we have already accomplished the first step. We selected the type of history we are going to construct when we decided to investigate the nearby history of education. We must next decide on the size and style of our study by defining our topic to make it manageable. Our "blueprint" consists of the questions we intend to investigate.

Developing plans for historical exploration requires two processes: defining the topic and developing the questions or issues to pursue. This chapter suggests a number of ways to define the work topically and poses a broad range of possible questions. Expect to begin modestly. Not even the most comprehensive history of nearby education could incorporate all the suggestions made here, and a nicely focused, clearly developed essay may embrace only few.

11

For those who are approaching the task of constructing history for the first time, what follows is critically important in providing a sense of direction and a focus for the investigation. We cannot simply forge ahead, collecting information on everything pertaining to education in our towns or counties, any more than we can attack a pile of bricks and lumber with no plans and expect to build a graceful townhouse. Keep in mind the suggestion in the first chapter that we must, in the nature of things, be selective in our histories. We cannot tell everything, and not everything is equally important. But we cannot know what is and what is not important until we define the topic of research and establish the issues to investigate.

Developing clear plans does more than allow us to eliminate certain categories of information, however. It also alerts us to material we might otherwise never notice. We could, for instance, collect information on the school's hot lunch menu, the number of businessmen who served on the local board of education, and the cost of window replacement in the elementary schools for the last four decades, but if our concern is to understand more clearly the position of the teacher in the school and the community, that material is of little value. If we are focusing on the social history of teachers and teaching, we may be alert to articles published by local teachers in state or regional professional teacher's journals, or we may watch more carefully for material that yields accurate data on average numbers of pupils per teacher over the years of study.

Defining Our Topic

You have, of course, already defined your topic to some extent by the very fact that you have decided to deal with the history of nearby education rather than with the history of the Peloponnesian War or changes in family size in Tioga County. But you still have an unwieldy topic, which can be focused more precisely. Will your research cover the entire sweep of history in your locality, from the training of the Native Americans before Columbus to the present? Will it embrace every mode of transmitting culture, from family devotions to rock 'n' roll stations? Will it treat every subject, from lists of library acquisitions, through fifth-grade field trips, to enrollment patterns in ethnic neighborhoods? No, obviously. You need to sharpen the focus.

There are three types of limits to consider imposing on your research. First, you may limit the study's chronological scope. If you are interested in formal schooling, you might focus on the entire span of time in which formal schools have existed in the locality, or you might select a narrower scope.

If you are studying a particular school or college, the chronological scope is limited by the years of that institution's existence, plus perhaps the period just before its founding, when the idea for the institution first emerged and was gestated.

Narrower limits may be suggested by other particular interests. If you wish to understand better the original purposes and uses of schools, for instance, you may limit the investigation to the schools' early years. If the focus is on the impact of urbanization on local schools, you may identify the era that embraced enough of the pre-urban history to give a sense of schools before urbanization and add it to the period of urban expansion and a period of mature urban life.

There are no limits to the ways in which you may assign periods to your historical research, but some make more sense than others. If you end a study of the impact of federal education initiatives on nearby schools in 1965, just as the Johnson administration's massive educational programs began to be felt, readers will have good reason to question your judgment.

You should justify to yourself and, eventually, to your audience, your choice of periods, for the rationale may not be self-evident. Michael Homel chose to write about Afro-American education in Chicago between 1920 and 1941, a restricted period that might seem strange on the face of it. But he had good reason to focus in this way. As he tells us in the preface to his study, the 1920s and 1930s

were especially important for black Chicagoans and the public schools. In 1920, there was substantial integration of black students and teachers, and schools that enrolled blacks were basically equal to the ones whites attended. By the eve of World War II, however, black pupils and instructors were rigidly segregated, and their schools received less money and were more overcrowded than those in white neighborhoods of varying economic and social status.

His focus on the interwar years, in other words, allowed him to study closely the dramatic segregation of a northern school system.

Second, you may need to define your research spatially. If you have decided to investigate one specific institution, you have already imposed spatial limits; otherwise, you need to determine how much of nearby education to embrace. Are you interested in the schools of an entire district? In all the educational institutions in a particular community? Will a township or county define the focus? Here again, a word of explanation to your audience may be in order.

Finally, you should define, at least provisionally, the topical limits of your research. The questions we will discuss momentarily will suggest the sorts

of topics that are available. Are you interested in local policy decisions or
in student culture, in changing extracurricular activities or the growth of
school bureaucracy? If you are concerned with questions of minorities in
the schools, will you include European immigrants or limit yourself to racial
minorities? Will your study of teachers include changes in the curriculum?
Are you more intrigued with secondary education than with elementary
or higher education, or will you include all formal institutions? If your study
focuses on a locality rather than on institutions—educational opportunities
in Scranton, Pennsylvania, in the nineteenth century, let's say—how broadly
should you cast your net? Will you include parochial as well as public schools?
Will you investigate the emergence of Sunday schools in mid-century? What
of the lyceum, that ubiquitous form of adult education that flourished from
the 1830s to the Civil War in northern and western cities, or the traveling
Chautauquas that brought high culture and famous lecturers to towns and
hamlets in the last quarter of the nineteenth century?

Clearly, you may focus in many ways. Having a sense of focus before you
begin helps enormously in directing you to the right sources and in allowing you to be more selective in collecting material. But while it is important to decide on the limits of a topic, it is also important to be flexible
about the limits. You may, in the course of your research, come across a
mountain of unexpected information on a topic you did not intend to include,
or you may come up empty-handed on an issue you hoped to tackle. Be
ready to change gears, to alter your strategy, to redefine the scope as you go.

Posing Research Questions

Once we have defined our general concerns in terms of time, space, and
topics, we can begin to develop more detailed plans by posing the specific
questions we want to answer. This process will begin to sharpen our focus
and keep us more clearly on track as we begin to collect data. To return
to the earlier analogy, we have decided upon the size, shape, and style of
our construction; now we will begin to sketch the blueprint.

For many people the stuff of history is the "firsts." Where was the first
school located? Who was the first teacher? What were the first books used?
How many attended the first high school? When we get beyond the "firsts,"
we tend to ask primarily *who, when, where,* and *what* questions.

Those are fine questions. We cannot begin to ask the more complex questions until we have the answers to those. If such questions define the range
of issues we are most interested in, we can gain a good deal of satisfaction

doing the detective work required to answer them.

There is another level of questions that we should give some thought to, however, to supplement those more traditional issues. They are the questions that seek to understand *how* and, particularly, *why*. It is interesting to know who the presidents of the local college were or to know when various districts consolidated into the present district. It can be valuable to know where various school buildings stood or what was studied in them. These are the building blocks to greater knowledge of our educational heritage.

That important knowledge becomes understanding and insight by reaching deeper, however. When we ask how the presidents of the local college were elected, why the small districts were consolidated, how the school sites were selected, or why the curriculum took on the precise form that it did, and, in each case, with what consequences, we are posing questions that require more information, more sources, broader methodologies, and more interpretation. And we are constructing history that provides more insight and gives more satisfaction. We can construct garages and remodel bathrooms and know that we are performing a valuable service. But we can also build homes, apartments, and estates. They take more time, work, and imagination, but they also provide greater satisfaction and perhaps add a greater measure of grace to the world.

Here I will discuss both the simpler questions, the garages, and the more difficult, the houses and estates. You decide which you can handle. They are presented here rather arbitrarily as questions about institutions, curricula, groups, ideas, and social foundations, but the particular issues you choose to research will doubtlessly not be limited to any one of those categories.

Institutions

What is the first thing that comes to mind when we think about the history of nearby education? Most of us think immediately of education in institutional terms. We think of buildings, classrooms, playgrounds, and institutional arrangements. We imagine early schools, log cabins, perhaps, or the little red schoolhouses from American mythology. We conjure up images of hickory-stick discipline and a lean, efficient curriculum, both wielded by selfless teachers.

Thus, the institutional aspects of nearby education provide a convenient point to begin an investigation. Some studies begin and end here; for example, a biography of a particular college, academy, or school is concerned primarily with institutional questions, though, as we shall see, even such studies

ELLEARDVILLE SCHOOL.

The Elleardville School, St. Louis, Missouri, in 1875, was a far cry from the one-room schoolhouse of nineteenth-century legend. A photograph such as this can yield many clues to questions about students, teachers, and schooling.

may profit from an enlarged scope. On the other hand, even if you intend to focus on other questions, it is wise to learn something about the particular institutional arrangements affecting your topic.

Many institutional questions are self-evident. If you are concerned with education in a community, district, or county, you want to know when formal education first appeared. In what ways did it grow and change? When did it go through the major periods of growth and change? What were the significant events in the history of the institutions, and why were they considered significant? Within the scope of your study, what sorts of educational opportunities became available, and what sports disappeared? What were the changes that came about? Who was responsible for founding schools or for changing them? When was a particular school or academy founded? What were the schools like? When were specific buildings built, remodeled, sold, or destroyed? How were the buildings used?

Histories of particular institutions are often primarily concerned with administrative matters. Who were the founders? Who were the presidents, headmasters, or superintendents? What were the administrative arrangements and patterns of leadership? How did individual educational leaders mold the institution? Indeed, many college and university histories are written as though nothing else mattered in the growth of the institution beyond the will and imagination of the presidents.

That is not to say, however, that an administrative focus is necessarily ill-advised. Much of value and interest can be gained from study of the administration of nearby education. How was educational policy determined, for instance? Who set policy—the superintendents, presidents, other trained educators, or governing bodies, such as boards of trustees or elected boards of education? What was the nature of educational leadership? Were the institution and its administrators bold or timid? Educational statesmen or followers? Propelled by educational principles or by fiscal considerations? When and how did the educational bureaucracy evolve? Why? With what consequences? What was the nature of change in educational leadership? For instance, where was control centered at various times in the history of the institution? When did the focus of control shift? How was it shared?

Perhaps even more interesting are the patterns of control and influence beyond the formal administrative structure of the institution. Alumni, businesspeople, benefactors, political groups, and other forces often wielded significant influence over the shape and content of education. Who attempted to exercise control over the board or the administration? What was their agenda? When were they effective, and when did they fail? What were the issues involved?

Many educational institutions adopt a formal "mission statement," a document that states the goals and aspirations of the institution. Even those without a formal statement have an implicit set of goals. What was the mission of the institution? Did it attempt to measure its achievement of the goals? How? What was the degree to which it achieved its goals? Were there contradictions between professed ideals and actual practice? How have the goals changed over the years?

Was the preferred form of discipline harsh or gentle? Were there debates or disagreements within the school or between the school and its patrons over the form and administration of student discipline? How did the disciplinary process fit with the mission of the institution? When and in what ways did discipline change?

What was the form or organization of learning? This may seem like a strange question for those of us who have gone through public schools, which have been effectively standardized throughout the nation, but there are many ways of organizing the learning process besides the sorts of classrooms found in most schools today. Was there an emphasis on rote memory? On listening and taking notes? On student involvement with learning? Were students encouraged to learn from one another? From the community? With others of the same age or with others of a variety of ages? Did the learning take place in a single classroom, or did students move from place to place to meet their teachers? Was the classroom the locus of most learning, or was there an expectation that children learn in the shop, the field, the street, and the home as well as—perhaps better than—in the classroom? What sorts of theories of learning and childhood were at work in designing the form of learning? If the subject is higher education, what ideals of the educated man or woman dominated the curriculum? When and in what ways did classroom practices change?

We have dealt thus far only with what actually happened institutionally. Were other options proposed? Might the institution have made different choices? What were "the roads not taken"? Why did the institution choose one option rather than another? I am not suggesting here that you get into the intellectual quagmire called "counter-factual history"—constructing an image of what might have been *if*. There is value, however, in discovering and analyzing the range of alternatives open to administrators, teachers, students, and communities at various points in time, in studying what we might call the "ideas in the marketplace." Which ideas were preferred. By answering that and by specifying what was rejected, you can better understand the decisions that were made and more clearly specify the consequences.

Now, to see the sparks fly, tie any or all of those questions together to ask *why*? Why was the institution founded? Why did it change in the ways it did? What were the justifications put forward at the time? Were there different justifications delivered to different audiences? Why? What were the publicly stated purposes? Were there other apparent purposes being served? Why did patterns of power and control change? With what consequences? Who benefited? Who lost? Why did certain purposes predominate at some times, and others at other times?

To begin to answer the *why* questions, you must engage in interpretation. You will see, as you begin to construct your history, that you must interpret evidence to answer nearly all but the most simple questions you have posed.

Curriculum

Curiously, historians of education have frequently failed to ask serious questions about the curriculum. What was learned and why?

There are three ways to get at those questions. The most obvious is through what historians and sociologists of education call the "explicit curriculum," the announced, printed, intended lessons. One need only ask obvious questions to discover the explicit curriculum. What subjects were taught? At what ages or levels? What was the content of the courses? What books were used? What sorts of visual aids were used? How was the material presented? When did the curriculum change? Why? What was added, and what was dropped? Who was responsible for curricular changes? What was the rationale for change? Was there any opposition? On what grounds? Did the curriculum fit the mission of the school? How much academic freedom did stu-

Notice the number of women participating in a class on engine repair and maintenance in night school at Soldan High School, St. Louis, in 1923. Such a photograph violates the expectations many people have about women's education in the past and reminds us to take nothing for granted in our research. Who received what sorts of education? When? Why?

dents and teachers have? What was the relationship of the content of the curriculum to the values and interests of the community and of the larger culture? Did the curriculum reinforce the dominant biases, or did it serve to counteract them, as Neil Postman suggests a proper curriculum should?

One of the things we know least about is what actually went on in classrooms. We know much about what various people thought *should* go on. Any number of people have been willing to unburden themselves on that subject. But how much of that actually affected teachers and students? Here the historian of nearby education can provide clues that researchers working at state or national levels cannot as easily produce. What was actually studied? Through what means? And what was learned? How effective were reform movements in terms of actually changing teaching and learning?

The second way we can discover what was learned is through the extracurriculum. We seldom think of extracurricular activities as part of the curriculum. After all, it is *extra*curricular, or outside the curriculum. How could it be part of the curriculum? It was fun.

The extracurriculum is sanctioned by the school, though. Those things we usually call "extracurricular activities" are school-sponsored or school-related and thus are, arguably, among the things the school sees as valuable and presumably related in one way or another to its mission. We probably learned as much, or perhaps a good deal more, from the extracurriculum than we did from the explicit curriculum, precisely because it *was* fun, and because it seemed to be freer of adult sponsorship than the classroom.

What, then, should we ask about the extracurriculum? We need to know what constituted extracurricular activities throughout the period of the study, how those activities differed for different age groups, when certain kinds of activities were added or deleted from school-sponsored activities, who participated in them, and the degree of adult intrusion. We may want to know, also, what sorts of activities young people engaged in outside the school before various activities were sanctioned by the school. As a single example, young men organized extensive sports leagues, which they ran themselves in many areas of the North, well before athletics were appropriated by schools and put under the control of adult coaches. What was the announced intention of the extracurricular activities? How were they funded? Who controlled them? How did students use them? Was there a status hierarchy of clubs and activities?

From such questions we can begin to interpret the role of the extracurriculum within the curriculum of the school by again posing the larger question: What was learned? Our concern must include, but also transcend, the obvious answers: athletes learned athletic skills, members of college literary societies strengthened their speaking and writing abilities, members of the drama club learned stage skills, student council members learned citizenship, Future Farmers of America learned hog judging. Beyond those, what was learned about autonomy, leadership, social class, sex roles, aesthetics, and the nature of the society? About intellect, self-worth, citizenship, work, and leisure?

The third avenue is through the implicit curriculum, or what some like to call the "hidden curriculum." The notion of a hidden curriculum comes from the sociological postulate that we learn not only from the purposeful teaching of churches and schools, but also from the unnoticed structures and forms of a society and a culture. For instance, Jonathan Kozol, among others, has suggested that young people, who are incarcerated in government-sponsored institutions for six hours a day for twelve to sixteen years or more of their lives at impressionable ages, learn acceptance of hierarchical authority structures, bureaucratized lives, and other features of modern life. Because we learn from the implicit curriculum by immersion in it, rather than by didactic teaching, we presumably do not notice the ways in which its teachings may contradict the explicit curriculum's lessons.

The implicit curriculum is the most difficult curriculum to deal with in historical research. Precisely because it is *implicit*—hidden, unarticulated, presumably unplanned—it cannot be studied directly. It can be revealed indirectly, however, and a historical investigation of it can be fascinating. Those who write about the implicit curriculum suggest that it is not simply haphazard, but rather that it reflects the needs and assumptions of the society. Looking at the schools historically, then, you may detect in the form and content of the hidden curriculum changes over time that mirror changes in the imperatives and values of the culture.

As you might guess, the debate over the implicit curriculum is fierce. Many writers in the last decade and a half have argued that the hidden curriculum of factory-like schools in the twentieth century is teaching students the accepted norms and expectations of an industrialized society—is preparing them, in other words, to be workers. Others, looking at the school through different lenses, counter that the democratic mass schools of the twentieth century teach the norms and expectations of participation as equal citizens in a republic. Only by carefully studying when, how, why, and for whom schools have changed can we begin to resolve that debate.

What are some of the indirect means available to you to identify and analyze the hidden curriculum? Some of the questions already posed will help you here if you are sensitive to the answers you discover. For instance, it is important to ask how the institution was organized. Were students and teachers confronted by an organization that stressed mutuality, equality, respect, and shared authority? Or by an institution based on hierarchy, segmentation, disequality, and top-down authority? Were learning settings structured to make students passive or active learners? Did students encounter adults as authoritarians who demanded respect or as authorities about knowledge and intellect who earned respect? Who controlled discipline? How was it dispensed? Was it dispensed impartially, or did boys receive harsher penalties than girls, poor student more than affluent students? What was learned as a result of each of those situations?

What messages did the culture, the ambiance, the atmosphere, of the school broadcast? Education in western culture is undeniably bookish, but how was that bookishness portrayed? Was it made as attractive to those who came from homes with little literary heritage as to those who came to the school already oriented to print media? What did young people think of the life of the mind and aesthetic sensibilities after attending the educational institution? What might students reasonably perceive the purpose of schooling to be as a result of their years in the institution? What might they have learned from teachers, not in terms of the explicit curriculum, but rather by what they saw of the teachers' attitude toward knowledge and intellect, by the degree of respect accorded teachers by the community? What was learned through each of those encounters?

And might the explicit curriculum and extracurriculum also have contained an implicit curriculum? What appeared to students to be sanctioned knowledge? What appeared to be appropriate leisure activities? What was left out of the curriculum? What did they learn about their world?

Groups

Isn't it curious that although education at its most fundamental level is the encounter between teachers and students, most histories of education have told very little about them? Pull down almost any article or book about education's history. You will learn a good deal about institutions, educational legislation, funding, even the books used and the lessons taught. Most wax eloquent about the "great men" (seldom the great women) who have fought

A segregated high school on Chicago's south side in the early 1940s. Racial segregation has been a dominant theme in the history of many schools that needs careful, uncompromising exploration. How did the explicit curriculum differ between white and nonwhite schools? Did students in segregated schools have access to the same extracurriculum? What was the implicit curriculum of segregation? Why were the schools segregated? With what consequences?

the good fight against ignorance—Horace Mann, Henry Barnard, John Dewey, and James Conant foremost among the warriors.

Nearby education does not usually afford us "great men" of that stature, but even historians of nearby education have focused on the prominent figures to the neglect of students, teachers, parents, and the rest of the community. Yet one of the great contributions that nearby history can make to an understanding of our educational legacy lies in the ability of historians of the nearby to turn the telescope around, to look at the everyday actors, to observe nearby education "from the bottom up." That can be done by looking at individuals and groups, trying to determine how the process of education actually worked, who benefited, and what actually happened in classrooms and hallways. The focus on a county, college, community, or classroom may not allow us to generalize about students and teachers in all places, but it does give us a sample about which we can speak knowledgeably.

A myriad of intriguing questions about various groups are available. Many of them suggest new ways of seeing the school and prompt new questions to ask of the institution and of its curriculum.

The historical study of groups draws heavily on the predominant concerns of social history. Social historians have been particularly interested to know how ordinary people lived their lives and have attended especially to differences in experiences between social classes, between races and ethnic groups, between age groups, and between sexes. Those categories of analysis are essential to extending our knowledge of nearby education.

Take students first. They are, after all, the ones for whom the enterprise exists. And perhaps no group has been more roundly neglected in historical studies.

Who attended the schools, colleges, academies, or literary clubs? For how long? Did more girls attend than boys? At what ages did they begin before the era of compulsory attendance? What groups tended to take the most advantage of the educational opportunities? Who most frequently quit early or never attended at all? Why? What were the patterns of attendance? For instance, in many nineteenth-century communities, young children often went to school in the summer, while the older students attended winter school. What might account for the attendance patterns? Were there changes over time in the patterns of attendance? What might explain those changes?

To what did they attend? Did all the children—boys and girls, workers' children and the children of the social elite, black and white—have the same curriculum, discipline, teachers, extracurriculum, and treatment? How did the structure of the curriculum differentiate between the sexes, races, or social classes? Were some curricular options chosen more often by one group than by another? If so, why? Because of advising, peer pressure, or school policy? What did the school or college offer each group in the way of extracurricular activities? Which group dominated in each activity? Did the institution or the students use the curriculum or the extracurriculum to underline class, race, or sex role differences? What were the patterns? How did they change over time?

What were the effects? What became of the students? How much of what they became in the future may we reasonably attribute to their education? How can we measure effects? What does each mode of measuring say about our educational priorities? Are there patterns of differences in the effects

Gender Differences in the High School Experience: 1920-1940

Traditionally, historians of education have been concerned primarily with ideas about education, educational policies, finance, and institutional change. Somehow teachers and especially students fail to appear in books on the history of education, even though a school without either seems strange indeed.

That is beginning to change as historians begin to pay more attention to groups usually left out of the historical picture. Questions are being posed, and new sources are being developed, to understand better the experiences of those who did not leave copious written evidence as did the thinkers, politicians, and school officials. The history of nearby education is particularly amenable to the new questions and new techniques, providing case studies that can be pursued rigorously and thoroughly.

Among the myriad issues now being explored, questions about the effect of gender on school experiences are attracting particularly keen attention. In this selection, Nancy Green demonstrates the sorts of insights that can be gained about changes in the ways boys and girls experienced high school. To uncover these changes, she focused on Chicago-area schools and used yearbooks and school newspapers as her primary evidence.

In the early 1920s, many extracurricular activities, including student government, school publications, debate teams, and cheerleading, were not identified as belonging to boys or girls, but in fact were dominated by boys. During the next two decades, girls gradually assumed a more active role in school publications, but most other activities continued to be either sex-segregated or, when mixed, were led by boys.

The most rigidly sex-tiered roles were positions of authority whether elected by students or appointed by school administrators. In student government, the president was invariably a boy and the secretary equally invariably a girl. In all circumstances where school administrators delegated authority to students, as in the case of hall guards or fire marshals, the students were male. Students recruited to help out in the office or library were almost always female.

In studying high schools in the late 1950s, James Coleman noticed what he called a tacit division of labor in most schools, with athletics being for boys and activities for girls. This division did not exist in 1920 in Chicago, but movement toward it did occur in the next two decades, especially in the case of school publications. In the 1920s, both girls and boys were involved in producing school yearbooks and newspapers, but the editor-in-chief was almost always male and the typists female. In the yearbooks of the 1930s, however, girls displaced boys as editors-in-chief, and by the end of the decade almost the entire staff was likely to be female. Boys maintained their involvement in school newspapers longer than in yearbooks, though girls gradually increased their share of newspaper jobs.

Writing, of course, was a field which had long been acknowledged to be appropriate for women, and there were just enough women in journalism to encourage girls to dream of it as a career. When Tuley High graduates of the class of 1939 put their "ambitions" next to their yearbook pictures, very few girls indicated a non-sex-typed goal (most wanted to be secretaries), but of those who did, more than half said they hoped to be a reporter or writer. In May 1923, Genevieve Forbes, billed as a "Star Writer" on the Chicago Tribune, *addressed students at Marshall High School, giving a talk that was "of particular interest to the girls." The following semester a girl was chosen as editor-in-chief of the school paper, substantially earlier than this occurred in other schools.*

Because males in the high school, as in the world outside the school, had higher status than females, all-male activities had higher status with both sexes than mixed activities. When girls began to participate in — or more especially to lead — activities that had previously been domi- nated by boys, boys soon lost interest in participating, not wishing to be involved in anything that could be said to be "for girls." This seems to have happened by 1940 to yearbooks. Between about 1935 and 1950 it happened to cheerleading. That it did not happen to school newspapers is undoubtedly owing to the domination of men in the profession of journalism. Yearbooks, as a purely school phenomenon out of touch with any adult enterprise, had no male status image and were more readily abandoned to girls.

Nancy Green, "Gender Differences in the High School Experience, 1920-1940," paper presented to the History of Education Society, 1984, in Chicago. Among other work on gender and schooling by Nancy Green, see "Female Education and School Competition, 1820-1950," *History of Education Quarterly* 18 (Summer 1978): 129-42.

of education? Did it, in other words, have the same effect on women as
on men, on working people as on the privileged, on ethnic groups as on
native born?

And how did students affect the institution? What was the student-created
culture of the school? Were there subcultures among the students? Was there
enthusiasm for or resistance against the efforts of the school and the teachers?
What did students expect from the school? Were there contradictions between the expectations of the institution and those of the students? What
were the traditions of the school? Were they created by the students or by
the teachers and administrators?

Some of those questions are relatively easy to answer. Others require
imaginative use of a broad range of sources. I will discuss later some of the
ways you may begin to seek answers.

What of the educators—the professors and teachers? We think we know
more about them as a group. The Ichabod Cranes held forth in schoolhouses
of the early national period and were later replaced by a more masculine
Hoosier Schoolmaster and, more frequently, by the New England school-
marm. We become less certain after the turn of the century. The teachers
were more professional, we think, but we have no clear image of them.

But are the earlier images accurate? Who taught? For how long? When
did women come to dominate what had for centuries been a male voca-
tion? How and why did that happen? At what age might a young person
begin teaching? How has the average age of teachers changed? What has
been the social class background, by and large, of our teachers? How has
their training changed? What have been the patterns of their careers? What
different profiles of teachers do we find at various levels of the educational
establishment, from kindergarten to the university?

What was it like to teach in the past? What was the quality of the
experience? What were the levels of monetary reward? Were there different
pay scales for black, brown, or white teachers, for male and female teachers,
for teaching different groups of students? What other rewards might a teacher
enjoy? What were the community's expectations of the teachers? What obligations were imposed? What sorts of professional activities were encouraged?
How active were the teachers in professional and in-service programs? Did
the teachers organize a teachers' union? How have the patterns of authority
and control affected teachers? How much control have teachers had over
the learning setting?

Has the institution sought actively to recruit and reward good teachers or to evaluate teaching? How has the institution responded to mediocre teachers? Have teachers had a voice in determining the quality of teaching or judging the competence of their peers? Have students? What factors encouraged good teaching? What factors perpetuated bad teaching? Is it true that teachers once enjoyed higher status in the community than they often do today? Did teachers once have a greater sense of commitment to teaching?

Those who are in charge of education are educators, too. Who has aspired to educational administration? Has the social, ethnic, or sexual composition of education leadership changed over time? Did change in composition alter the patterns of leadership? How did leaders attain their position? How have they, as a group, differed from teachers? How have their jobs changed over the years?

Finally, the community itself deserves attention. We have already asked questions that will reveal which sectors of the community availed itself most fully of the educational system, and which benefited most. We need to understand better the attitudes of community groups toward education, however. Has a hesitancy to become involved with the school system indicated hostility toward education, apathy, intimidation, or resistance? What evoked the hostility, apathy, intimidation, or resistance? In other words, does the observed attitude reflect anti-intellectualism, fear of cultural imperialism, ignorance, opposition to increased taxation, or something else?

Who had the greatest influence on the institution? What groups have been represented most often on the school board or board of trustees? How did the community affect the schools besides through the electoral process? How effective have organizations such as the parent-teacher associations and college alumni associations been? What can be determined about the community's philosophy of education, its sense of the purposes of school? Has its philosophy changed? When? Why?

Ideas

A perennial debate among historians and philosophers concerns the role of ideas in historical change. Do people and institutions change because of a particularly good idea, or is change propelled by social and material forces beyond the influence of ideas, good or bad? Probably your work in nearby history cannot answer that question, but it is an intriguing one to deal with in your work. What ideas did people appeal to when they sought to defend what education was doing or to attempt to encourage it to do something else? Were the ideas original, or were they derived from other sources—a contemporary national dialogue, perhaps, or traditional educational values? What social forces were at work to resist or accelerate change? Which seems to carry the greater weight in explaining the results of the struggle? Were the ideas advanced merely ad hoc justifications for what was happening or deeply held commitments? Can you even adduce a fair answer to that?

One way to begin to unravel that last problem is to listen carefully to the ways in which those who articulated ideas expressed them to various constituencies. While all speakers tailor their messages to their audiences, you may suspect the integrity of speakers who advanced one set of purposes for education before a group of workers and a contradictory set before the local

Salute to Froebel   Divoll Kindergarten.

Children and teacher participating in a 1904 "Salute to Froebel" at the Divoll Kindergarten in St. Louis, Missouri. By comparing a photograph such as this with early handbooks on kindergarten methods, one can reconstruct a great deal about what the atmosphere of an early kindergarten must have been like. Note the decorations on the wall and the statue of Froebel. The balls hanging from the ceiling, while at first difficult to identify, are among the pedagogical devices developed by Froebel to teach children to discriminate differences in color and shape.

chamber of commerce, for instance. What was said? By whom? To whom? What hidden agendas might the speakers have had? Were the ideas internally consistent? Were articulate alternatives advanced? By whom? With what effects?

Social Foundations

On the other side of the ledger are economic imperatives, political decrees, and social factors that influence education. We might call these intangible but powerful forces the "social foundations" of education. How have the social foundations affected nearby education? How did changes in the social class composition of a district affect its schools? What accommodations had to be made during periods of economic reversal? Were changes in the ways people worked reflected in the mission and content of schooling? In what ways? How were perceptions of social change—declining strength of families, say, or increases in political unrest, crime, or social deviance—dealt with by the institutions? What sorts of social problems was education expected to resolve? How? Was it successful in dealing with those problems? What efforts were made to monitor its ability to do so?

Being Sensitive to Context

Recall the illustration of history as a series of concentric circles. The most recent set of questions, those dealing with ideas and social foundations, emphasize that nearby education does not exist in a vacuum but is a part of a larger context, a smaller circle within the larger circles of the state, the nation, and the world.

Our focus is on the nearby. But if the history we construct is to have any value in extending understanding, we must remain acutely aware of the larger structures within which nearby education grew. No matter how we have defined our topic, the institution we are studying was, in some way, influenced and shaped not only by nearby events but also by regional, national, and international events. Therefore, we need to ask what was going on historically during the period of our study. What were the political trends? In what directions were the region, the state, and the nation moving economically? Where was education heading? Were there changes in families, in the nature and rhythms of work and leisure, in immigration or race relations, or in the roles of men and women? Constructing the history of nearby education may well be a means to understand and appreciate history more generally, for nearby history shows more naturally the relationships between our own circles and the larger circles that surround us.

Being aware of the larger educational and social contexts of particular historical interests is vital to unraveling the most difficult and most interesting question we can pose, the *why* question. As argued earlier, the *who, when, where, what,* and *how* questions are important and interesting and require some interpretation, but *why* demands the most interpretation and hence requires the broadest understanding. *Why* have Americans placed "most of their hope for social order in the basket of public education," to quote Stanley K. Schultz? *Why* did the periods of educational reform occur when they did? *Why* did schools adopt the corporate model of bureaucratic control? *Why* were schools so frequently anti-intellectual? *Why* did the extracurriculum develop in the ways it did? *Why* have we moved from one form of education to another? Ultimately, *why schools?*

Difficult? Yes, but a fascinating and satisfying endeavor, too. Perhaps that is because, as the French historian Marc Bloch once remarked, we are "stimulated far less by the will to know than by the will to understand." So, somewhere in your plans, add a few challenging *why* questions.

Recall the admonition earlier in this chapter: you cannot possibly attempt to answer all the questions posed here. What you should have by now is a clearer sense of the precise topic you are going to tackle and an interim list of the questions for which you want answers. Those make up your rough plan. They will guide your search for sources and your collection of information. Just remember as you move on that these are an interim list and a rough plan. You need not tie yourself to a rigid blueprint as the carpenter might do. Remain flexible, open to new questions, altered focuses, and revised objectives.

Suggested Readings

Many of the questions and ideas suggested in this chapter are inspired by recent work in the new social history. For a good general introduction to what is meant by the term, see Peter N. Stearns, "The New Social History: An Overview," in *Ordinary People and Everyday Life: Perspectives on the New Social History,* edited by James B. Gardner and George Rollie Adams (Nashville: American Association for State and Local History, 1983), pp. 3-22. The other essays in the volume deal with particular issues in the new social history—race and ethnicity, gender, urban and rural life, families, work and workers, and so forth—which are of concern to the historian of nearby education. See also Stearns's review of recent work in the field, "Toward a Wider Vision: Trends in Social History," in *The Past before Us: Contemporary Historical Writing in the United States*, edited by Michael Kammen (Ithaca, New York: Cornell University Press, 1980), pp. 205-30; and Clarke A. Chambers, "The 'New' Social History, Local History, and Community Empowerment," *Minnesota History* 49 (Spring 1984): 14-18.

I have quoted or drawn illustrations from the following in this chapter:

Michael W. Homel, *Down from Equality: Black Chicagoans and the Public Schools, 1920-1941* (Chicago: University of Illinois Press, 1984), p. x.

Neil Postman argues, "The school stands as the only mass medium capable of putting forward the case for what is not happening in the culture," in *Teaching as a Conserving Activity* (New York: Dell Publishing Co., Inc., 1979) p. 22.

The implicit curriculum is discussed in Jonathan Kozol, *The Night is Dark and I Am Far from Home* (Boston: Houghton Mifflin, 1975) and several of his other books. See also, for example, John I. Goodlad, *A Place Called School: Prospects for the Future* (New York: McGraw-Hill, 1984), pp. 226-45.

Stanley K. Schultz used a case study of nearby education to understand better this society's penchant for transferring the solution of all social problems to the schools. See *The Culture Factory: Boston Public Schools, 1789-1860* (New York: Oxford University Press, 1973), p. xi.

Marc Bloch, *The Historian's Craft* (New York: Vintage Books, 1953) provides some philosophical reflections on historical studies by a mid-century historian.

Nancy Green's reference to James Coleman is from his *The Adolescent Culture: The Social Life of the Teenager and Its Impact on Education* (New York: Free Press, 1961), p. 15.

·3·

Detective and Historian

ROBIN W. WINKS, AN AMERICAN HISTORIAN, SUGGESTS
that historians are much like detectives. There is a good bit of the sleuth
involved in the search for evidence and the construction of an explanation
and interpretation. To collect and make sense of the data concerning nearby
education, one must, like Scotland Yard, explore every possible source of
information, follow each clue, and even use a healthy amount of intuition.
Much of the delight of historians' work, in fact, lies in the detective work
that must go into gathering the material for their stories. Not a little of
the frustration lies there, too.

Where do historians do this detective work? What do they look for? This
chapter and the next two are intended as guides to the searching process.
This chapter points out the most likely places to visit in the search for clues
and evidence and how to deal with the material found. Chapter 4 discusses
the more common, or at least more traditional, sorts of evidence available
in those places. Chapter 5 turns to materials that are less commonly thought
of, less used, and more unconventional. It also discusses the ways to use
that material or the questions one can answer with it.

You may not be able to use all of the suggestions made here and may not
need to visit all of the possible sources of evidence. The scope you have
chosen for yourself, and the questions you wish to answer, will determine
to a large extent how much of this material you need to locate. Moreover,
once you begin your detective work, you may find other sources I have not
mentioned. This discussion, like the book as a whole, is intended to point
you in some likely directions, not to serve as a fail-proof recipe.

Where to Look

Agatha Christie's Inspector Poirot seldom found evidence in the same place from case to case. Your search will not take you nearly as far afield, but the scattered nature of the evidence for the history of nearby education will probably surprise you. My efforts to locate historical material on schools in towns and cities across the nation have often called for perseverance and ingenuity. The material is seldom in predictable places.

Unlike many governmental agencies that periodically send various records to state or national archives, public schools in most states are under no obligation to do more than to preserve, usually locally, a very few records having to do with students, building construction, financial matters, and personnel. Small private and parochial schools may have kept even less. Only colleges, academies, and large parochial systems, such as the Catholic schools, seem to have much concern for the careful collection and preservation of records that are of value to historians.

As a result, you will frequently have to look in out-of-the-way places, and occasionally you will have to piece your story together with fragments of evidence. Constructing the story of nearby education is not a simple matter of a trip to the local school offices. But the search for fugitive records, lost files, and unconventional sources is part of the detective work that makes historical research enjoyable.

Usually the best place to start the search is at the local or county historical society. Not only will you find some of the material that I will discuss here and answers to many of your questions, but you are likely also to gain support and encouragement. People who work in the over nine thousand historical societies and museums around the country are, like you, interested in their heritage and in presenting it to their communities. Usually their first obligation is to the careful preservation of the materials turned over to them and to presenting visually some of that material in a museum or displays. Less frequently do they have the staff or funds to engage in more detailed research and writing that leads to literary presentations. For that they must depend on the efforts of researchers like you.

Thus, you will probably find at the historical societies people who know your community, who know where much of the material you seek may be found, who will have some of that material in the societies' collections, and who, because of their shared interest in telling the community's story, will usually provide a wealth of information. Cultivate them well, and heed the suggestions I will make later about using historical materials. The historical society staffs may become your most important resource, even if their collections hold little of direct value to your investigation. Detectives have always known the importance of informants.

What are you likely to find at the local or county historical society? The possibilities are endless. The organization may be primarily a museum with little in the way of manuscript or library collections. In that case, there may be little of specific relevance, unless part of the museum display or the collection of artifacts includes material objects from the local educational institutions. But even in historical societies with limited resources, I have found society members who were remarkably knowledgeable about the schools. They knew who the teachers were, when they had taught, where the schools were located, who had packets of letters about schools, where the school

---

Primary and Secondary Sources

Historians and other scholars in the social sciences distinguish between "primary sources" and "secondary sources," and since I use that terminology here, a definition may be appropriate.

Briefly, a primary source is any material created contemporaneously to an event being studied. A secondary source, on the other hand, is an account created subsequently, usually by a historian or other scholar using a number of primary sources. For instance, if our subject is the history of a local college from its founding to 1960, the speeches of the college's presidents, the records of fraternities, issues of the local newspaper, the alumni office's files, and published material, such as a volume of student reminiscences or a pictorial history of the college, all constitute primary sources. But the history of the founding years of the school written by a student as a master's thesis in 1934 and Professor Graham's *Our College in the Growth of American Higher Education* are secondary sources.

Primary sources are not limited to printed material, as we shall see in Chapter 5. Photographs, buildings, trophies, and all other materials that tell us something about our subject and that were created during the period we are concerned with constitute primary sources. Both primary and secondary sources are of value to us, though we clearly wish to rely much more fully on original testimony — primary sources — than on other writers' interpretations of that testimony.

board minutes of defunct school districts had ended up, and so forth. Society members are likely to know with whom to talk for oral history interviews or may be likely candidates for some recorded reminiscences themselves.

You may be more fortunate, however. Only a thirty-minute drive from where I sit now, there are three county historical societies, each with a remarkable array of educational material in its collections. Were you to visit them, or any of the thousands of others like them, you would find teachers' scrapbooks, photograph collections including pictures of educational institutions and school activities, and manuscript collections of various sorts pertaining to educational issues. The societies have copies of nearly all the local newspapers from the earliest volumes and copies of the counties' manuscript censuses. One of them has a good collection pertaining to a private academy, which flourished from the 1820s into the 1870s, including class lists, catalogues, and engravings of the academy's main building. Each society has scattered official records from the area's public schools, copies of school textbooks, and such ephemeral material as report cards, diplomas, teaching certificates, and merit awards.

County historical societies are frequently the best places to begin the search for historical sources. Though they vary greatly in resources, many have records of various sorts pertaining to nearby education. The one-room schoolhouse, left, located in Morton, Minnesota, is the home of the Renville County History Society. Though modest, the society houses excellent primary source documents on education in the county. The Clinton House, above, home of the DeWitt Historical Society of Tompkins County, in Ithaca, New York, is a fine example of a well-funded, comfortable museum and research center.

One county historical society museum in Minnesota has a display cabinet devoted to the history of the local college. The display makes a good beginning point for a local researcher. In addition to a number of photographs and material artifacts, the cabinet contains a good collection of early yearbooks and catalogues from the college. Another county society in Minnesota uses two well-preserved one-room schoolhouses as its historical museum. That group has a remarkable number of valuable items, including official manuscript records—attendance registers, school clerks' books, teachers' reports from ungraded schools, and annual reports to the state superintendent of schools.

Libraries are another important source. Occasionally, a local library holds manuscript material one might expect in the historical society collection, particularly when there is no active historical society or when the society does not have the resources to create archives. Frequently, too, public libraries have complete runs of area newspapers and may have an unpublished index to one or more of the newspapers. A tiny town library I visited, located

The following is a complete census of all children between six (6) and sixteen (16) years of age residing in School District Number **2** _Sibley_ County, Minnesota.

Dated _September 20,_ 19 34

NOTE: Enter age of each child as of October 1st of the current year. Illustration—A child past seven who will become eight years of age after October 1st shall be listed as seven years of age. A child who reaches his sixteenth birthday on or before October 1st of the current year shall not be listed.

Make a mark (x) at the left of the name of each child under eight years of age as of October 1st.

Fill in and sign certificate on other side of this blank. Send a copy of this report to the County Superintendent of Schools not later than October 1st.

	NAME	SEX M F	DATE OF BIRTH Month Day Year	Age Oct. 1	Name of Parent or Guardian	POST OFFICE
1	Barke, Richard	M	Sept 21 1919	15	Wm Barke	Henderson
2	", Earnie	M	May 10 1922	12	"	"
3	", Meta	F	May 10 1925	9	"	"
4	Carlson, Betty	F	Aug 6 1924	10	Mrs. Mary Carlson	"
5	Doerr, Milfred	M	Feb 5 1919	15	Wm Doerr	"
6	", Mary	F	Dec 10 1921	12	"	"
7	", Erwin	M	Dec 5 1923	10	"	"
8	", Lucille	F	Feb 7 1926	8	"	"
X 9	", Harvey	M	Oct 1 1927	7	"	"
10	Hoffmann, Mary Alice	F	Apr 15 1926	8	Wm Hoffmann	"
11	", Rita May	F	Apr 15 1927	7	"	"
12	", Theresa Ann	F	Aug 1 1928	6	"	"
13	Kroehler, Linda Joy	F	Oct 30 1924	9	F. P. Kroehler	"
14	", Lorin	M	Apr 10 1926	8	"	"
15	", Allen	M	Apr 10 1926	8	"	"
16	Kroehler, Joan	F	June 7 1928	6	R. H. Kroehler	"
17	Lieske, Ruth	F	Nov 21 1919	15	F. A. Lieske	"
18	", Walter	M	Oct 6 1918	15	Mrs Henry Lieske	"
19	", Karl	M	Aug 12 1926	8	E. H. Lieske	"
20	", Harriet	F	Nov 19 1927	6	George Lieske	"
21	Meyer, William	M	Feb 12 1921	13	Wm Meyer	"
22	", Lester	M	July 6 1922	12	"	"
23	", Marvin	M	May 17 1924	10	"	"
24	", June	F	June 30 1927	7	"	"
25	Miller, Marvin	M	Apr 13 1924	10	Ed. Miller	"
26	", Geraldine	F	Dec 5 1927	6	"	"
27	Schultz, Iney	F	Oct 12 1926	7	Aug Schultz	"
28	", Floyd	M	Sept 24 1928	6	"	"
29	Teach, Earl	M	Aug 10 1921	13	Ernest Teach	"
30	", Sylvan	M	Feb 14 1923	11	"	"

☞ Before filling out this report study carefully EVERY direction on the fourth page.

TEACHER'S ANNUAL REPORT TO THE COUNTY SUPERINTENDENT
UNGRADED ELEMENTARY (RURAL) SCHOOL

District No. 61 _____ County of Sibley _____, Minnesota

YEAR ENDING JULY 31, 1934	Boys	Girls	Total
I. School census and compulsory attendance law. (Census includes all children 6-16.			
11. Number of children 8 to 16 years of age included on census who have during this year attended public school only - - - - - - -	4	6	15
12. Number of children 8 to 16 years of age included on census who have during this year attended private or parochial school only - - -			
13. Number of children 8 to 16 years of age included on census who have during this year attended part of the time in public schools and part of the time in private or parochial schools - - - - - - -			
14. Number of children 8 to 16 years of age included on census who have not attended any school during this year:			
141. For whom written excuses have been issued by the board - -			
142. For whom no excuses have been given - - - - - - - -			
15. Total number of children between 8 and 16 years of age (Ages 8 to 15 inclusive) included in school census for 1933. (Sum of 11, 12, 13 and 14) - - - - - - - - - - - - - - - -	4	6	15
II. Apportionment.			
21. Number of pupils entitled to apportionment (see directions, 4th page)	12	9	21
22. Number of pupils not entitled to apportionment - - - - - -			
23. Total number of pupils enrolled (sum of items 21 and 22) - -	12	9	21
III. Enrollment by ages.			
31. Number between 5 and 8 years of age enrolled (ages 5-7 inclusive)	3	3	6
32. Number between 8 and 16 years of age enrolled (ages 8-15 inclusive)	9	6	15
33. Number between 16 and 21 years of age enrolled (ages 16-20 inclusive) - - - - - - - - - - - - - - - - - - -			
34. Number pupils under 5 and over 21 years of age enrolled - - -			
35. Total number of pupils enrolled. (All ages.) - - - - - -	12	9	21
IV-V. Enrollment by grades.			
42. First Grade - - - - - - - - - - - - - - - -	2	1	3
43. Second Grade - - - - - - - - - - - - - - -	2	2	4
44. Third Grade - - - - - - - - - - - - - - -	2	2	4
45. Fourth Grade - - - - - - - - - - - - - - -	2	1	3
46. Fifth Grade - - - - - - - - - - - - - - -	1		1
47. Sixth Grade - - - - - - - - - - - - - - -		2	2
48. Seventh Grade - - - - - - - - - - - - - -			
49. Eighth Grade - - - - - - - - - - - - - - -	3	1	4
51. Ninth Grade - - - - - - - - - - - - - - -			
52. Tenth Grade - - - - - - - - - - - - - - -			
53. Eleventh Grade - - - - - - - - - - - - - -			
54. Twelfth Grade - - - - - - - - - - - - - -			
58. Total number of pupils enrolled. (All grades.) - - - - -	12	9	21
VI. Attendance.			
61. Total attendance in days by all pupils - - - - - - - -	X	X	3417¾
62. Total days of school including holidays (Length of term in days) -	X	X	180
63. Average daily attendance (divide item 61 by 62) - - - - -	X	X	19
64. Average number of days each pupil has attended (divide item 61 by 23) - - - - - - - - - - - - - - - - - -	X	X	164.5
VII. Number of pupils entering school this year for first time - - - -	2	1	3
VIII. Number eighth grade pupils graduated - - - - - - - - - -			
	Men	**Women**	**Total**
IX. Teachers and instruction.			
91. How many teachers of each sex? - - - - - - - - - -		1	1
92. Total wages of all teachers in this school for ONE month - - -	$	$ 45	$ 45
93. Has instruction been given, as required by law, in:			
931. Morals and effects of narcotics and stimulants - - - -		yes	
932. Physical and health education - - - - - - - - -		yes	
933. Citizenship, including the Constitution and Declaration of Independence - - - - - - - - - - - - - - -		yes	
X. Has the United States flag been displayed as required by law? - - -		yes	

The county courthouse is frequently an important repository of sources for the history of nearby education. Among the sources located in the Sibley County Courthouse in Gaylord, Minnesota, are school census returns, maps indicating the location of schoolhouses, periodic reports from school clerks and teachers, and county commissioners' records. I found the school census returns in file cabinets sharing a closet with the air-conditioning equipment.

in a former church, yielded a full run of the local high school's yearbooks
and a large pasteboard box with a partial run of the school's student newspaper, play programs, and printed material from proms, banquets, and other
student activities.

Don't stop with the public library, either. School libraries may have yearbooks and school papers, records of library acquisitions, and evidence of
changing tastes in student reading habits. School authorities sometimes
entrust official records to the school librarians, despite their perennial lack
of funds or space to care adequately for them.

Local college and university libraries are worth a visit as well. Even if you
are not going to include higher education in your study, talk with the librarians at the college. They frequently have archives connected with their institution; some include material relevant to your work. Be aware of the many
ways higher education has been involved with public schools during your
visit to the local college or university. Higher education has long served
as a teacher training center, a source for curricular innovation, and a center
for evaluation. The college may have sources that will give you an entirely
different view of the local schools.

Both public libraries and school libraries may have secondary sources for
your study—the books, theses, and articles written by other historians and
researchers about your topic. Do not rely solely on the standard library aids,
such as the card catalogues, the indexes, and so forth. Librarians are resources,
too. Often they know about a published source that you may never stumble
across. For example, when I was working in the Stevens County Historical
Society library recently, the librarian dug out an article from a 1917 issue
of the *American Review of Reviews*. Entitled "City Comforts for Country
Teachers: A Minnesota Neighborhood Sets an Example to the Nation," the
article described the accommodations provided for the teachers in a tiny
hamlet in the county. Even if that article is indexed somewhere, I would
have been unlikely to have thought to search for it in the course of my
research into the history of Stevens County's schooling. Yet here in a national
magazine was interesting information.

Depending on the questions one is concerned with, the county courthouse may be on the research itinerary. My own study of public schooling
in Coconino County, Arizona, required more hours in the courthouse than
in any other single location. Arizona, like several other states, provided county
superintendents to oversee the small districts that could not afford their own
superintendent. The superintendent's office was located in the courthouse

and turned out to be a rich source of material. County courthouses frequently hold handwritten minutes of the county board of supervisors, school censuses, maps noting location of schools, clerks' and teachers' reports, school land patents, and other information on public schooling.

It is natural to think first of the school district offices as a source of material for a history of nearby education. While you will certainly visit those offices, they appear late on this list. I have found that, surprisingly, public schools keep very few important records. Most keep only those records that are required by law and routinely destroy all other material within a few years of its creation. Thus, while you may hope for files of correspondence, directives on policy issues, minutes from faculty and administrative committees, evidence on the theories of education affecting school policy, or data on research, you will be fortunate, indeed, if you find much beyond the required records on individual students and staff, along with the school board minutes.

Even major city school districts fail to think about preservation of valuable historical records. Recently the Pittsburgh school system discontinued its research office. The office's files, doubtlessly rich sources of historical data on a variety of educational and social issues, were discarded. As Carolyn Schumacher remarked, "The evidence of fifty years of local educational trends and theories was thereby lost."

If the superintendent is relatively new to the district, he or she may not be aware of what is available. After gaining permission from the superintendent to use school resources, therefore, it is wise to talk to several people in the school about your project. Secretaries and janitors are particularly apt to know where files have been stored over the years. Look beyond the office vault and files, if possible. Valuable information has turned up in attics, broom closets, furnace rooms, and bus garages. In a community near me, a former clerk of the school board has school board materials from several decades in her home. She was told many years ago that the school did not want the items cluttering up its offices and that she could dispose of them as she saw fit. Fortunately, she held onto them, and, fortunately for me, a worker at the county historical society knew of their whereabouts. The moral: Talk to everyone.

If your interest is in private or parochial schooling, the public school offices usually have little of value. If the schools you are interested in are still in operation, then probably they have useful records in their own offices. You may find records on nonpublic schools in the offices of county or state superintendents. Parochial schools are often easier to trace than private schools, at least in those cases where the church had a strong central office to oversee its schools. Consult the diocesan archives and the record offices of the major denominations, either in person or by correspondence.

This does not exhaust the places you should visit by any means. Check the local newspaper office for clipping morgues and back issues of the paper if they are not available elsewhere. Look for individuals who may have personal papers they will allow you to peruse, particularly school board members, prominent students, teachers, administrators, or laymen active in local educational affairs. Visit or correspond with the state archives or the state historical society. You may be rewarded richly. If the state department of education has deposited its papers at one of those institutions, or if you can consult those papers at the offices of the department, you may find many reports filed by the school you are researching or special reports on the schools of your community written by the state staff. Finally, get in touch with the local parent-teacher organization, student groups, and teacher associations to gain access to their records.

Every community has its own peculiarities when it comes to the location of information on education, and the list here is not exhaustive. Search broadly. I am told that dozens of boxes of records from the Binghamton, New York, public schools turned up in an abandoned city incinerator, no better for water and rodent damage, but largely intact. Learning where to look is part of the detective work and part of the fun.

The Search for Fugitive Files

Source material for nearby education's history is likely to show up in unpredictable places. None of us, working by ourselves, can expect to locate all that is available. Thus, it is important to let many people know about our projects, as Platt Cline discovered during his research on the history of Northern Arizona University.

It was expected that another fruitful source would be minutes of governing boards, but while those of the Board of Regents that assumed control in May 1945 were complete and available, the only minutes for the boards of education that governed the school in earlier years consisted of records of meetings covering only twenty-one months in 1921-22. No one on the campus could say where, if indeed, anywhere, could be found the remainder of the records.

A search through stacks and boxes of records in the basement of the administration building brought us to a file drawer labeled "Board Minutes," but it was empty. Further search seemed useless, but business office employees who had shown interest were asked to watch for letter-size sheets in loose-leaf or post binders, similar to those which had survived.

To reconstitute the minutes from other sources, we obtained from [Arizona State University] archives copies of minutes of the board which had governed both Normal schools in 1899-1901, copied abstracts of minutes that had been published in the Sun *and the* Gem *between 1901 and 1912, and from the state archives recovered some minutes from files of former superintendents of public instruction between 1915 and 1945. We now had records of about 30 percent of the boards' meetings, sufficiently scattered over the forty-six years to provide insights into affairs under a variety of members and during many changes, and the writing of this history proceeded.*

Then in 1980 a campus accountant, Victor H. Pereboom, digging through business office records, came upon a very large leather-bound book of the kind used in early days for financial records and which, for that reason, had been pushed aside in the search for minutes. Idly turning the stiff pages, he found he had the original handwritten minutes from April 1, 1901, through 1912. In the fall of 1981 another accountant, Clyde N. Shreeve, his interest honed by Pereboom's find, uncovered a long-buried, locked cabinet, searched until he found a key which fitted, and opened the drawer to reveal minutes covering about twenty-five years, filed and forgotten when the Board of Regents took over in 1945. The minutes are now complete except for about eight years, the gaps being 1913-19 and 1927-29.

The file of catalogs in the archives lacked eight issues from the school's first sixteen years. Providentially, Mrs. Clarine Gillenwater, a regular attendant of garage sales, spotted a bundle of pamphlets that she recognized as old Normal school catalogs, and her find made the collection complete.

Platt Cline, *Mountain Campus: The Story of Northern Arizona University,* (Flagstaff, Arizona, Northland Press, 1983), pp. 373-4. (© 1983, by Platt Cline.)

Using Historical Material

I will turn, shortly, to a more thorough discussion of the sorts of material we may find in our research and what we may be able to make of the evidence unearthed. Before doing that, however, allow me to offer a few suggestions about using archives and other repositories and about handling evidence.

Return a moment to the detective analogy. Both in real life and in fiction, detectives must be scrupulously careful with all clues and evidence. That material is not only important to their own immediate task of solving a puzzle, but important also to the courts, the press, and ultimately the public. Other individuals and agencies must be able to evaluate independently the detectives' findings to judge accuracy. Detectives must be careful not to obliterate fingerprints or lose painstakingly located hair samples. They must accurately record the location of each item of evidence. They must not suppress a single scrap of evidence. They must conduct their interviews in such a way as to be welcomed back at another time. They have, in short, an ethical obligation to the public and to posterity to be thorough, courteous, careful, and accurate.

The issue is no different for historians. They, too, work under ethical obligations. They must be as careful with their evidence as detectives, for others must be able to verify their accounts, by examining the same evidence they used, or to turn to that evidence to ask other questions of it. Historians must record accurately what the evidence says in order to report it accurately and must note carefully the source of the evidence. They must comport themselves in offices and archives in such a way as to ensure they will be welcomed back and that those who follow them will also be welcomed.

What does that mean specifically? It means, first, that, as reseachers we need to observe a few rules when we physically handle historical documents. Keep in mind that many of those documents are one-of-a-kind. If they are soiled or destroyed, there are no others to replace them. Many have become fragile with age. Always handle them with clean hands, and handle them gently. Be particularly careful with old books and documents, like newspapers, that have been bound together. Old paper is frequently brittle and can break easily at the binding. Call any damage to the attention of an attendant. Use microfilm copies when available.

Always use pencils or a portable typewriter, not pens of any kind, when working around manuscript documents. An accidental pencil mark can be erased from a page (let the attendant do that task); an ink mark lasts forever.

Many repositories will photocopy material for you for a small fee, thus allowing you to take exact replicas away with you and saving you a good deal of time while on location.

When working with loose papers, keep them in the order in which you received them.

And never remove anything. There is little that is more distressing to historians and archivists than stolen or mislaid manuscripts and other historical material. Don't abuse the trust someone has put in you by giving you access to historical documents.

Whether you are working in a school principal's office, college archives, or private collection of papers in someone's home, be a good guest.

Finally, be extremely careful to document the exact location or source of every item you find. The same accuracy expected in footnotes referring to printed sources is expected in footnotes referring to manuscript and other sources, though the format is different. Handbooks, such as Kate L. Turabian's A *Manual for Writers*, provide specific instructions on the technical issues of citing primary source documents. The general rule is to provide all the information on a source that would be needed to enable other researchers easily to locate the document themselves. That information includes the author, if known, identification of the document (title or label if it has one or generic name—letter, scrapbook, diary, etc.—if it does not), date if known, and physical location. To ensure accuracy, devise a consistent system of noting manuscript sources before you begin.

You now have a plan in the form of a clear topic and a list of specific questions. You have an idea of the places to look for material. But what specifically should you look for? What can you do with it?

Suggested Readings

Robin W. Winks provides entertaining and lively insights into the problems encountered in evaluating and interpreting history in The Historian as Detective: Essays on Evidence (New York: Harper and Row, 1968).

The story of the Pittsburgh school district's destruction of research office files is told in Carolyn S. Schumacher, "Using Board of Education Materials for Local History," Western Pennsylvania Historical Magazine 66 (January 1983): 84-90.

For suggestions on the correct ways to document historical sources, see the relevant sections of Kate L. Turabian, A Manual for Writers of Term Papers, Theses, and Dissertations (Chicago: University of Chicago Press, 1971), or Frank Freidel, ed., Harvard Guide to American History (Cambridge: Belknap Press, 1974), particularly the section entitled "Research Methods and Materials," pp. 3-134.

·4·

Hearing Voices from the Past

DOCUMENTS ARE HISTORIANS' BUILDING MATERIAL, the sources of their clues and evidence. Customarily we associate the idea of a document with paper sources, such as a handwritten letter, an inscribed proclamation, or a book. There are, however, many other types of documents. "A document is recorded information in any form," according to Kyvig and Marty. "Whether the information is handwritten, typed or printed on paper, etched on glass or metal, carved on wood or stone, or impressed on film, audiotape, or computer disk, it speaks of its moment of origin."

Printed documents have long provided historians with their primary source of historical data. That has been changing in the last couple of decades. Increasingly, historians have turned to other types of documents to learn more about the past. This chapter focuses on print documents, both published and unpublished. The next chapter introduces a wide variety of less conventional documents.

I do not mean to imply that one sort of document is superior to another. They all have potential value. Presenting the sources in this way merely makes the discussion of the various types more manageable. The discussion begins with more familiar documents, sources that you perhaps are already somewhat adept at evaluating and interpreting, for you handle newspapers, letters, books, and other forms or print communication nearly every day. After familiarizing yourself with these common forms of historical documentation, you will turn with greater confidence to other documents, print and nonprint, that can deepen your appreciation and understanding of history.

Establishing the Context

It is frequently wise to begin by learning all you can about the general "lay of the land." What is already known about the subject, if anything?

47

Whether you are writing a general account of public education in your community or a specialized study of the professionalization of local teachers in the Progressive Era, you will avoid a lot of backtracking (there will be enough of that anyway) if you know early in the research such things as the general chronology of events, the actors, and the significant places.

There are two levels at which to work in this first stage of research. Both require research in secondary sources. At the most obvious level, find out what research has already been done on the community's history. Do not limit yourself to what others have written on local education. Rather, try to gain a broad sense of the development of the community. Education does not develop in isolation; it develops within an environment. Thus you need to find out from the secondary sources—the books, articles, pamphlets, theses and dissertations written about aspects of your community's history—when things happened, how, to whom or what, where, and why. When, for instance, did ethnic or minority communities develop? What was the effect of economic depressions on local workers? Who was responsible for the cultural growth of the city? Where were the schoolhouses located, and why?

Such information makes the work in the primary sources easier by giving you a sense of chronology and an introduction to at least a few of the pertinent events and historical actors you will meet more directly in the primary documents. It also provides some arguments to test and some facts to verify.

It is possible that no one has yet done any writing on your nearby history. The task becomes more difficult in that case, but not impossible. You will be breaking new ground. It would be well, in that case, to see what has been written about adjacent towns, the county or region, and the state. All will shed some light on the specific development of the area you intend to write about.

The second level of work in secondary sources is one historians of community institutions often neglect with unfortunate consequences. It is important not only to know the local context in order to understand better the particular issue being investigated, but also to gain at least a general acquaintance with the larger universe in which the community and its education developed. That does not mean that you must master all of the thousands of history books in the library before you begin to research or write local history. It means merely that you will profit from spending a few evenings with a selection of general histories and, particularly, good histories of education in your state and in the nation.

With a grasp of the general flow of events in the historical development of education and the sources of those events beyond the school walls, you will appreciate the reasons for the sudden burst of reform activity in your community from the turn of the twentieth century to the war years, or the movement away from a Latin-based curriculum to a more science-dominated course of study in your community's college in the last quarter of the nineteenth century. You will know that those events in your community were part of similar movements throughout the nation at the time. You will also be in a position to recognize innovation or resistance to national trends. You will, in short, be better able to evaluate and interpret the history you uncover. You need, in other words, to understand the *context* of the history you intend to research and write about.

You need not complete a review of all secondary sources before moving on to what is, for most of us, the most challenging and exciting part of research. Gain a general sense of context, then begin to work in the primary material, pursuing the secondary reading as the project develops.

There are no precise rules on the next step, but generally it makes sense to turn early in the research to newspapers. A survey of the local newspapers during the period of the study brings to life many of the issues you have read about in the secondary source research. If there are few or no secondary sources to rely on, newspaper research may be the first sustained, chronological introduction to a community's history.

Newspaper research may take substantial time. If your locality was served by rival papers during all or a portion of the period you are studying, you may find it helpful to survey all of them to observe different viewpoints. In some instances, it may also be worthwhile to read through the files of larger regional papers for any mention they might make of your topic.

A survey of local newspapers should not be limited to the mainstream press. A century ago a much richer variety of newspapers flourished than we have today, written for specific audiences. Many immigrant ghettos in American cities boasted their own papers, usually in the language of the homeland. Similarly, the diverse political movements that thrived from the 1880s until the First World War spawned both national and local newspapers intending to foster populism, grangerism, labor unionism, socialism, and other political causes. These usually differed markedly in outlook and interests from the mainstream press. Both mainstream and fringe papers may be important sources for historians of nearby education, for education has often been seen by immigrants, socialists, populists, Afro-Americans, and the labor movement as the key to their own advancement.

If students in the institution you are researching published their own news-papers, pay careful attention to them, too. College papers are almost always valuable sources. Newspapers from secondary schools are sometimes frus-trating, however. Some schools, at certain periods in their history, had good journalism teachers and serious student editors. But many student papers may seem, in retrospect, embarrassingly silly and gossipy. Yet you can use even these thoughtfully to probe aspects of student culture, and the better papers tell much about teachers, learning, and youth.

The idea of facing a year of newspapers, much less fifty or a hundred or more years, is enough to take the luster off the endeavor. It is a large task but usually manageable and nearly always worth the effort for the informa-tion to be gleaned. And there are ways to streamline the process.

For instance, almost without fail, publishers established a consistent pat-tern in the organization of their papers. News items on local education are likely to show up in the same general part of the paper from year to year. On the relatively few occasions when an educational issue caused a stir in the area, the news of that issue might make the front page. Generally, however, education news is more likely to appear elsewhere in the paper, along with other issues of purely local interest. Once you have a sense of the publisher's priorities, you will find that you can scan the headlines on the appropriate pages at a good pace. Then, too, certain times of the year elicited more interest in education than others. You may want to read more carefully newspapers issued around the beginning of a school term, during periods of school board elections and budget votes, and near commencement time. If you are interested in gauging opinion on educational issues, watch the editorial pages and the letters to the editor.

Furthermore, a few papers have been indexed. If you have cause to believe that the indexing was adequately comprehensive, you can probably rely on the index in your search for items on specific events, people, and ideas. Some of the big city dailies have published indexes. Other indexes may still be in typescript and may not be widely available. Those must be tracked down. I have used a few indexes that were assembled by the New Deal's Works Progress Administration, the WPA. These indexes were still on the original three-by-five cards, handwritten, filed in shoe boxes, and gathering dust in the corners of libraries. Ask around. Finally, in some instances, old news-paper morgues and clipping files have survived. These were bulky files, usually consisting of hundreds of manila envelopes identified by individuals, places, and issues. Into them went relevant clippings from each day's paper. They, too, can save time.

While indexes and other shortcuts make the research more efficent, an issue-by-issue march through the local papers has its benefits—you develop a keener sense of the life of the community and a greater sensitivity to the interrelated forces creating the patterns of nearby history. If you read only the articles dealing directly with the annual fate of the school budget, for example, you might miss the crucial economic and demographic changes in the community that affected the budget votes. Likewise, relying on clippings or indexes may cause you to miss the advertisement for a private business college that flourished in the town for two decades, an institution that the newspaper never commented on, but whose records may still be available and whose work extended nearby educational opportunities.

Be forewarned, however, that newspaper research sometimes takes you far afield if you let it. It is easy to get caught up in the news of events unrelated to your topic. While working on the history of education in a frontier community some years ago, I found myself spending whole afternoons immersed in stories of bank robberies and the subsequent tales of posses, clues, gunfights, arrests, and trials, all stretching out over several months of front-page headlines; or intently following the saga of the efforts by the Industrial Workers of the World to organize local miners. Neither promoted my search for evidence about the development of local educational institutions, although both enriched my sense of the context in which those institutions developed.

Ferreting out Other Published Primary Sources

At some time or another, nearly every locality had a newspaper, which may serve as a valuable source. There are numerous other print sources to look for, though few are as universal as the newspaper.

Many schools and virtually all colleges published catalogues listing their course offerings, faculty, and sometimes the names of the students enrolled. Some distributed faculty and student handbooks, which detailed the rules and policies of the institutions. Frequently both sources included formal statements of purpose or brief histories of the institutions. With such material, we can begin to trace changes in curricular emphasis, with due regard to pomposity and public posturing, to examine notions of the purposes of education. Linked to other documents, these items allow us to gauge the extent to which public statements of educational theory matched actual practice. Changes in school rules and policies provide fascinating insights

CATALOGUE

OF THE

OFFICERS AND STUDENTS

OF

CORTLAND ACADEMY,

HOMER, N. Y.

FOR THE ACADEMIC YEAR,

1857-58.

HOMER
JOS. R. DIXON, PRINTER.
1858.

INSTRUCTORS.

STEPHEN W. CLARK, A. M.
PRINCIPAL.

MISS HARRIET S. GUNN,
PRECEPTRESS.

MARINUS N. ALLEN, A. B.
INSTRUCTOR IN LATIN AND GREEK.

FREDERICK R. DOWNES, A. M.
INSTRUCTOR IN MATHEMATICS.

MISS HARRIET TAYLOR,
INSTRUCTRESS IN MODERN LANGUAGES.

BERNARD M. DEWEY, M. D.
INSTRUCTOR IN NATURAL SCIENCES.

MISS SARAH A. PAYNE,
INSTRUCTRESS IN THE ENGLISH DEPARTMENT.

MRS. MARY LUND,
INSTRUCTRESS IN MUSIC—INSTRUMENTAL AND VOCAL.

ALMON R. BENEDICT,
INSTRUCTOR IN PENMANSHIP.

STUDENTS.

GENTLEMEN.

Names.	Residences.
Elias C. Ackerson,	Niles.
George A. Adams,	Skaneateles.
Walter R. Adams,	Killawog.
Warren W. Babcock,	Apulia.
Willis G. Babcock,	Homer.
Isaac T. Babcock,	Homer.
Augustus Bacon,	Spafford.
Nelson M. Baker,	Lafayette.
William Ballard,	Cortland.
Augustus Ballard, Jr.	Cortland.
Charles W. Bancroft,	Scipio.
S. McClellan Barber,	Homer.
Benonijah M. Barber,	Spafford.
Augustus Bennett,	Homer.
Isaac J. Bennett,	East Homer.
Grenville R. Benson,	New York.
George M. Berry,	Borodino.
Deston F. Bingham,	Camillus.
Joseph Bishop,	Cortland.
William H. Black,	Homer.
Dennis Boden,	Scott.
William Boies,	Homer.
Edward E. Bostwick,	Onondaga.
James L. Bothwell,	Groton.
Martin I. Bottrill,	Otisco.
John W. Bowen,	Homer.
William Bradley,	W. Greece.
Alvan Bradley,	Clovert.

HOMER ACADEMY

AND UNION SCHOOL.

1873-4

BOARD OF INSTRUCTION.

CHARLES H. VERRILL, A. M., - - Principal,
And Teacher in the Classics, Natural Sciences and Higher Mathematics.

Miss LOTTIE M. HITCHCOCK, - - First Assistant
In Academical Department and Teacher in French and German.

JOSEPH ATWATER, - - - Grammar School.

————— ————— - Intermediate Department.

Mrs. A. TORREY, - - - Primary Department.

Miss EMMA WATROUS, - First Asst. in Primary Department.

Catalogues from nineteenth-century academies, such as these from the Cortland Branch of the Rensselaer School in the 1830s and from the Homer Academy, 1873-1874, contain much less information than their modern counterparts, but used creatively, they can provide valuable insights into the institutions they represent.

into changing ideas about education and perspectives on the dynamic relationship between social change and educational change. We may innovatively use the lists of faculty and students in ways I will explore more fully in the next chapter.

Ever since the era of professionalization, dating roughly from the last quarter of the nineteenth century, organizations of professional educators have published a great variety of material. Historians have used much of the material produced by the national organizations, but the pronouncements, policies, and pleas published by the local and regional counterparts of the national societies have been neglected. What were the teachers in McMinnville, Oregon, discussing at their quarterly meetings in the 1920s? Who controlled the agenda at the yearly "teachers' institutes" in Wisconsin's rural counties? When did educators in Gunnison, Colorado, first begin hearing about educational progressivism? What was the response of Rockville, Illinois, teachers to the militant unionism of their Chicago colleagues in the early years of the twentieth century?

We may approach these and a multitude of other questions through a variety of material published by overlapping local groups of educators. Most schools of all sizes had teachers' organizations of some sort, often associated with a state and national society. In some areas, county associations provided rural and small town teachers with the sense of professional membership. Administrators, who sometimes belonged to the teachers' associations, insisted on touting their special professional expertise through their own professional societies as well, often with local or regional groupings. In the largest districts and in colleges and universities, we may frequently find local chapters of subject area associations and learned societies.

Most local educators' associations published at least a newsletter and occasionally a more substantial journal. During the heyday of professional grouping, educators published the proceedings of annual regional institutes, superintendents' days, conferences, and state conventions. Do not overlook the journals of the state educational associations in your search for information on nearby issues either. Some carried news of the local chapters. Nearly all periodically surveyed conditions in various parts of the state. Most encouraged articles from members, so the chances are fairly good that you will find one or more contributions by educators from the institution or locality with which you are dealing. Some of those articles speak directly about issues, research, or practices relevant to the questions you are pursuing. At a minimum, the state educational associations' publications extend your sense of the larger educational context.

Chief school officers and governing bodies at a number of different levels publish periodic reports—headmasters, college presidents, boards of trustees, superintendents, state departments of education, and the federal education agency, among others. Since many of these reports are required by law, most have probably survived in one form or another. The most relevant, obviously, are those closest to the focus of your research—reports of local officers and boards—but do not neglect higher level offices. Churches with systems of academies and colleges usually have boards of overseers appointed to maintain general oversight for the schools. Their reports to bishops, general assemblies, or other church bodies contain information on the individual campuses. Boards of trustees report regularly to the public or to the body that appointed them.

State education departments and the state superintendents of instruction concern themselves with local educational affairs because of their responsibility to gather statewide statistics and to monitor compliance with education law. They report regularly to the legislature, and those reports contain specific information on local education. State departments must also intervene in unusual cases and often submit special reports. The periodic reports of the state education departments are indispensable sources of quantitative data on nearby education, particularly if the local manuscript reports from which the state reports were compiled have not survived.

There are other sources of published primary sources as well. Active parent-teacher organizations publish brochures and newsletters. Locate the records of the local organization if possible, for both published and manuscript material. From time to time, various local civic, service, labor, and business groups take an active interest in local education and publish tracts, pamphlets, and position papers designed to influence teachers, voters, or the school board. Any hint you find in a newspaper or other source that the chamber of commerce, the machinists' union, or the grangers took a stand on a local school issue should send you scrambling to find independent historical evidence.

Do not neglect the maps you find hanging on office and historical society walls, bound together in large volumes, or filed away in various places. City, village, township, and county maps often indicate the location of schoolhouses. Many of the popular commercial maps of the last century featured engravings of prominent houses and civic buildings, including the local schoolhouses. Such maps may provide views of school buildings that may have been destroyed or remodeled and may indicate the existence of schools for which all other evidence has disappeared. A series of area maps from various periods of time documents the growth of the school district, the pattern of consolidation, and the geographical distribution of school buildings.

Obviously, maps are valuable for locating abandoned school buildings. Many are still around, altered beyond recognition, perhaps. They find new life as community halls, homes, apartment houses, hay storage sheds, churches, and other adaptive uses.

A creative search may turn up still other printed sources. At times of apparent crisis for young people, for instance, a host of agencies have launched studies of the "youth problem" or the "crisis in the schools." The early twentieth century, the Great Depression, the mid-1950s, the late-1960s, and the early-1980s were particularly rich periods for studies of youth and schools. Those studies tell us volumes about students and schools and the problematical relationship between the two. Such a study might have been conducted in the school or district you are researching.

Likewise, teachers, administrators, districts, schools, and academies have been the targets of independent investigations at various time. Whether by accrediting agencies, sociologists, journalists, or other educators, the reports generated by those studies, if they can be found, provide a more analytical approach to the history of an institution than can be gained easily anywhere else.

Many of the sources noted so far are available only for the last one hundred years or less. Published material on education is much less plentiful for the first two-thirds of the nineteenth century and nearly nonexistent for the Colonial origins of nearby education. However, print evidence is only a start. I will turn next to material we might find in manuscript.

Manuscript Sources: Reading Other Folks' Mail

I sometimes wonder if other historians have the same feeling about manuscript material that I do, or if this is my private perversity: As important as printed evidence is, I still prefer to work with old handwritten documents. There is something coldly formal, or perhaps very public and common, about the printed word. But a private diary, the smudged, penciled pages of a minute book, an 1867 letter to a teacher in North Carolina—there is the warm flesh and blood of history. Or maybe I just get a thrill out of reading other people's mail.

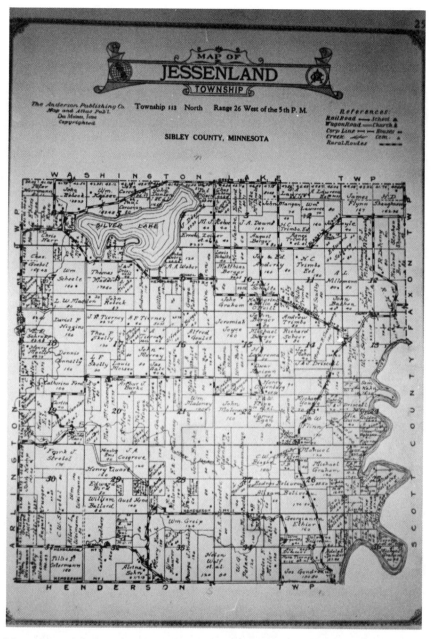

Maps suggest much about the development of education and changes in children's experiences in attending school. This map of Jessenland Township indicates that six schools served the area in the 1920s, none more than two miles or so from any of the rural residents. Today there are no schools left in the township. The farm children of Jessenland Township are bussed as much as an hour one-way to one of three consolidated districts. How does that change affect the experience of schooling for the children of the area?

Using Depression-Era Youth Studies
in Local Educational History

The 1930s were one of several periods in which the problems of young people generated special studies. The reports resulting from those studies included verbatim interview responses, clinical profiles, and quantitative material about youth in that period. These youth studies are of interest to the historian of nearby education because they focused on the youth of particular towns, cities, counties, or states. Hence they are, as Jeffrey Mirel writes, "a virtual gold mine of information for local educational historians," if we locate one that was based on the youth of our locality. Here is how Mirel describes the studies and their uses.

As unemployment for young people between the ages of 15 and 24 reached nearly 50 percent, double the estimates of adult unemployment, communities became increasingly concerned about how their young people were weathering the storm. By 1935, communities across the country were hiring psychologists, statisticians, and interviewers to investigate what the popular press had labeled the "Youth Problem." Between 1934 and 1936, more than 120 local youth studies were completed. Many more were to follow.

These studies are still easily accessible. Many of them are listed in American Youth: An Annotated Bibliography *by L. A. Menefee and M. M. Chambers (1938). Copies of the studies may be available in nearby research libraries, through interlibrary loan, or possibly in the files of local boards of education. Some studies received funds from federal programs, particularly the Works Progress Administration, so a letter to the National Archives in Washington, D.C., might turn up a local or county survey.*

The quality of the studies is uneven. They range from Howard Bell's classic survey of more than 13,000 young people in Maryland, Youth Tell Their Story *(1938), to surveys of a small number of high school students obviously written on an inadequate budget. Some progressively recount the experiences of more than ten years of high school graduates, while others look at a single group of young people at a fixed point in time. Nevertheless, these studies do share some common features. Most rely on extensive interviews with their young subjects. In their own words, youth tell about the difficulties they had finding jobs, their experiences in school (especially concerning the value of vocational education), their reasons for leaving school if they had dropped out, and their attitudes about a host of social problems and issues.*

Among the exciting discoveries researchers may make in the youth studies are unexpected data to answer questions the researchers did not even think to pose. One good example is the material found in En Route to Maturity, by Ray Johns (1938), a survey of youth problems and youth services in Detroit. In his discussion of the services provided by the National Youth Administration (NYA), Johns includes information about the IQ scores of 2,000 NYA youths, with additional information about the scores of 200 black youths and 200 youths whose parents were foreign born. Researchers could use these data to question some assumptions scholars currently hold about IQ testing. For example, most scholars believe that the IQ tests used in the early part of this century were culturally biased to favor native-born, white, middle-class children. Yet the range of IQ scores from this sample of young people, all of whom were from families on relief, matched the normal distribution for the city generally. The scores for the black youths and for those of foreign-born parents were also distributed normally. While this is hardly a knock-out case against the notion of culturally biased IQ tests, it is challenging and provocative.

In some cases, we may even be able to go beyond the published studies and work with the raw data themselves. While the chances are probably slim for uncovering the complete interview schedules used for the studies, a search for them could turn out to be extremely rewarding. A researcher who found the actual schedules would be able to recode and reanalyze the data in order to answer questions that the interviewers in the 1930s were simply not interested in. For example, it might be possible to answer questions about relationships between ethnicity and early school-leaving or socioeconomic status and vocational education.

The youth studies of the 1930s are a wonderful, though untapped, resource. Through them we can begin to hear the voices of young people in our research. They can be invaluable in doing local educational history.

Jeffrey Mirel created this selection especially for this volume. He used youth studies in his "Politics and Public Education in the Great Depression: Detroit, 1929-1940," dissertation, University of Michigan, 1984, and in Jeffrey Mirel and David Angus, "Youth, Work, and Schooling in the Great Depression," *Journal of Early Adolescence* 5 (October 1985): 489-504.

Be that as it may, working in manuscript records is an important part of constructing any history. Printed sources reveal what someone or some group intended to convey to a large group of people—a committee, the legislature, members of a professional organization, students, or the public at large. Manuscript material, on the other hand, was more often expected to be private, whether as notes to oneself in a personal journal, comments to a friend in a letter, or records intended for a specific and limited audience, such as minutes of a committee or confidential personnel records. Such items tend to be more candid, less guarded, than public pronouncements or contain material never obtainable in published form.

A major source of manuscript material is the records of the institution you are studying. As indicated in Chapter 3, much that you might hope to find in the files of many schools has long since been destroyed, and not all that is extant will be in the school offices. Still, barring the constant problem of destruction by fire or other natural disasters, there may be, at a minimum (for the last century, at least), such things as board minutes and confidential records.

The minutes of the board of trustees are often spartan and prosaic. Usually they record only final action on issues, not the content of debates, disagreements, or battles. Occasionally, however, they record roll-call votes, allowing one to trace trustees' alignments on issues. Generally the minutes serve as a source of relatively accurate dating, a means for verifying certain facts from other sources, and, for colleges and school districts lacking extant business records, as a source of financial information—salaries, costs for materials, and so forth.

Used sensitively, however, minutes of boards yield other valuable insights. Viewed broadly, they provide, for instance, one barometer of shifting priorities and perspectives on education. Or, in the case of public school boards particularly, they illustrate the changing power of the board over time. A researcher needs to take careful notes on how the board voted on issues that recurred regularly or to watch for the sorts of issues the board had within its purview from decade to decade. Did the patterns of votes reflect pressure from various groups? Did the arrival of a new major employer in the community affect attitudes toward vocational education? Did a period of economic prosperity result in changed curriculum or financing that might reflect an altered outlook on education? Did the superintendent's power *vis-a-vis* the board change over time? You may pursue these and other questions in part through a careful reading of the minutes of the board.

Student and staff records are sources that remain underused by historians. Traditionally, these records have been used for simple quantification—how many students enrolled each year, how the faculty-student ratio changed, what the salaries paid to teachers and administrators were, and so forth. Student records, in many cases, divulge information on secondary school and college curricula. While catalogues and course listings tell us what courses were available, from the student records we may discover which courses were actually taken by the majority of students. I will return in the next chapter to talk about other ways to use these materials.

Other interesting quantitative data can be gleaned from the ubiquitous reports submitted by teachers, superintendents, clerks of the board, and others. I have stumbled across dozens of these forms, tucked away in historical society collections, private papers, and school files. Those dating from the 1860s through the 1940s are fascinating for the information they include on a curious collection of concerns: condition of privies, use of flagpole, size of school library, quality of classroom ventilation, number of students vaccinated, number of visits to the school by the school board or the county superintendent, along with monthly enrollment, average daily attendance, days missed for inclement weather, and number of months the school was in session. We learn not only about the school itself, but about the sorts of issues that preoccupied the bureaucrats who designed the forms.

Some correspondence files may be available, particularly from private schools and colleges, along with the private papers of teachers, superintendents, and other individuals. Depending on the sources of the correspondence, the range of information available is nearly endless. Teachers may have commented on aspects of their work; those involved politically with education may have expatiated at length about their views on education; administrators may have made any number of remarks about the schools, the teachers, the students, and the community.

Among other manuscript material created by schools, look for admissions books, treasurer or business office records, discipline reports, records of the steward and butler (in older colleges and academies), teachers' lesson-plan books, examples of students' work, school censuses, and records of graduates. Watch also for indexes to help with a search for school records. In at least a few counties in the country, the WPA in the late 1930s conducted searches for all extant school records and created index files that listed the location of the records at that time, their conditions, inclusive dates, and capsule summaries of the chronology of each district in the counties. The

CLASSIFICATION AND SCHOLASTIC PUPIL RECORD

District No. 28   Teacher Marcella B. Miller   Term Ending June 2 19 33

	Group pupils according to grade. List advanced grade pupils first						YEARLY AVERAGES					

KEY OF GRADING
A—Excellent, 93 to 100
B—Commendable, 86 to 92
C—Average, 81 to 85
D—Passing, 75 to 80
F—Failure, Below 75

Pupil Number	PUPILS' NAMES	Age	Grade in School	Total days Attendance	Kind of Credit	American History	Arithmetic	Geography	Grammar and Composition	Reading	Elementary Citizenship	Hygiene-Sanitation	Spelling	Penmanship	Promoted to what grade	Retained in what grade
1	Lothes, Bernard	16	8	143	Local	86	87		77	86		86	94	86	9	
					State	Pen	Bvd		Pen	Pen		Pen	Pa8			
2	Wilkinson, Lionel	14	8	150	Local	79	78		84	75	83	81	81	82		8
					State	F70	C84		F60	C80		F02	P80			
3	Bartz, Grace	13	7	141	Local	80	82	82	84	83	78	79	84	85	7	
					State		F62			F64	F71					
4	Wilkinson, Chrystal	12	7	160	Local	82	81	84	85	86	80	82	93	83	7	
					State		F60			85	F00					
5	Bartz, Arnold	10	6	122	Local	68	75	75	73	82		84	75	87	not	
					State											
6	Brown, Larry	6	1	135	Local		95		96	95		95	96		2	
					State											
7	Schiffler, Dick	6	1	159	Local		99		96	92		90	95		2	
					State											
8	Whelston, Bernard	7	1	142	Local		80		78	78		75	77		2	
					State											
9	Whelston, Charlotte	6	1	154	Local		89		85	68		78	78		2	
					State											
10					Local											
					State											
11					Local											
					State											
12					Local											
					State											
13					Local											
					State											
14					Local											
					State											
15					Local											
16					Local											
17					Local											

Virgil & Vernon Chalcraft did not
come the whole year therefore I
did not give them final averages

1. Is daily program posted upon wall? *Yes*
2. Have you received School Census? *Yes*
3. Are you following State Curriculum? *Yes*
4. What time do you reach school each day? *7:45*
5. Times teacher tardy .... Reasons ....
6. Are you a member of the State Education Association? ....
7. What Educational Journal do you take? ....
8. What professional work are you doing? ....
9. Educational meetings attended during the month? ....
10. Have you assisted in a community project this month, and what type? ....
11. What wall decorations are you using this month? *Halloween, Columbus, Indian*
12. Has the Flag been displayed in accordance with law? *Yes*
13. Do pupils know Flag salute? *Yes*
14. Are you giving health instruction? ....
15. Have you inspected toilets each week? *Yes* Condition of boys' toilet *air*

Condition of girls' toilet *fair*
16. Is toilet paper supplied? *Yes*
17. Have you a supply of sanitary towels and basin? *Yes*
18. Are pupils required to wash before eating lunch? *Yes*
19. Do you have hot lunch equipment? *Kettle + pan*
20. Is water supply adequate? *Yes*
21. Is fountain filled each day? *Yes*
22. If school is to be closed in the near future, give time and cause *Thanksgiving*
23. How many circulars and letters have you received from the County Superintendent's office this period? *Two*

24. Supplies needed *Daily Marks Book*

Catherine Dolan
Teacher.

Various monthly and annual reports, required over the years, were usually submitted on printed forms. Left: "Classification and Scholastic Pupil Record," 2 June 1933; above: "Teacher's Report to County Superintendent," 193?, both from Renville County, Minnesota. What sorts of questions can we answer if we locate such records covering a period of several years? Will they be of more value than records for a single year?

indexes I have found consisted of the original handwritten or typed index cards as they were created fifty years ago. Many of the records I have used were in the hands of individuals when the search was conducted, and some may still be found in family collections.

This is a good place to insert a word of caution about the use of this and all other historical material. Some of the material mentioned above includes confidential information about school grades, age, nationality, income, and a variety of other issues. Clearly, there is always the possibility of embarrassing individuals or their families, at the least, and even liability on the part

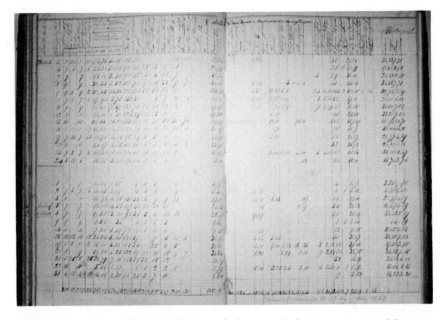

The types of manuscript school records you may find vary greatly from state to state and district to district. Comprehensive records, like the one above detailing the condition of all the school districts in a central New York State township in 1849, are all too rare and frequently must be pieced together from disparate sources. This remarkable volume, labeled "Records of Cortlandville School Districts, 1830-1946," was found in the Cortland County, New York, Historical Society library.

of the researcher. Indeed, some offices and archives are loath to provide access to confidential material much more recent than, say, fifty years, as a means of ensuring confidentiality. To protect yourself and the individuals named in student and staff records, it is essential to use confidential material as aggregate data and to avoid naming individuals in relation to information taken from confidential sources.

Village, township, city, and county boards have also been involved in educational decisions, especially concerning school taxes, and their minutes and other manuscript sources are valuable. If possible, talk to the current clerk who has responsibility for the records. This individual uses the records frequently for legal purposes and has a good sense of the sorts of information available.

You may find some manuscript sources even farther afield. Research on parochial schools or church-related colleges and academies suggests seeking access to the ecclesiastical archives of the church in question.

Write to the archives before traveling to them. Questions of resources, access, and working conditions are better dealt with in advance. It is frustrating to arrive at archives to find that they do not have what you want, are not open, or will not let you use a camera, typewriter, or other equipment. If the distance to the archives is prohibitive, a letter of inquiry may still be fruitful. If eccesiastical archives have particular documents or short collections of material you need to see, they may photocopy the material and send it to you for a reasonable price. Others may make the microfilmed portions of their collections available through interlibrary loan. Microfilms and other resources may be catalogued in published pamphlets available for a nominal cost.

Similarly, manuscript material on public schools often ends up in the state archives, the archives of the state historical society, or in the files of the state education department. As noted earlier, manuscript returns or required state forms from nearby schools may still be available, often containing information not distilled into the published annual or biennial reports of the state agency. The state agencies also frequently keep correspondence files better than the local districts do. Letters from local superintendents, principals, and other officials to the state officers and copies of correspondence from the state to the local districts may well be housed in a state agency today. Again, a letter of inquiry is wise before investing in a trip.

Since state departments of education have oversight of all the school districts in the state and act as arbiter in many states, unresolved local educational disputes and questions of education law are appealed to the departments or their chief officers. If necessary, the departments may launch an investigation. Because of the nature of the cases, the reports are usually confidential and unpublished, but the manuscript reports, providing information not readily available anywhere else, are usually still in the files.

Finally, seek out private manuscript collections. Retired teachers, superintendents, headmasters, board members, and former students are all possible sources of evidence. Some have carefully saved personal documents pertaining to nearby schools. Whether saved for sentimental reasons, as part of a professional collection, or for some other reason, such collections can be priceless, and many of the people who have them are thrilled to know someone finds them of interest. Ask all of your contacts—librarians, older teachers and professors, the staff of the local historical society—about private collections. The network of people who know about your research is

Nearby History in Church Archives

For some questions and topics, the records of churches that ran nearby schools or colleges are vital. Most denominations maintain archives, and local ministers, priests, or nuns may be able to supply you with addresses if you wish to visit the archives or write to inquire about particular records.

The Roman Catholic Church maintains more collections than any other American church and has also had the most extensive parochial school system. Tracey Mitrano, who has used various Catholic archival collections, describes the sorts of material available and the experiences she has had in her work. Although other churches do not have as much material nor all the same types of material, these comments may apply to many other ecclesiastical collections.

A wealth of historical information on local education exists in the archives of Catholic institutions. Diocesan archives, usually the most well-organized and catalogued, contain materials concerning the founding of the diocese — deeds, correspondence, the personal records of church leaders, or unpublished accounts of the founding process. In addition to these materials, the diocesan archives are also the best source of correspondence sent to the prelates of the diocese, and in some cases, there are even copies of correspondence sent from the diocese as well.

The headquarters of religious orders usually have similar kinds of materials plus the most valuable piece of information in their archives: the chronicles of the order. These chronicles functioned as the community diary, were written anonymously, and record the events, impressions, and details of daily monastic or convent life. College archives hold a full spectrum of collegiate artifacts, including correspondence, college reports, annual bulletins, yearbooks, and alumnae and alumni records. The quality of organization of these materials differs with each college. Catholic primary and secondary schools may also have a collection of materials, although they are much less likely to be catalogued formally. Information about the history of these schools can also be found in diocesan records.

Accessibility to these records varies and depends on the type of office, the nature of the request, and the personality of the archivist. I have been told that problems I had in obtaining materials were to be expected because "even the Catholic Church has original sin, you know." I have also experienced delaying tactics, where it has taken a few to several inquiries to set up an appointment. On the other hand, most archivists could not have been more helpful or cordial. Not only did they open their archives to me, but they also opened their doors. In one case, I was the privileged guest for a week at a convent where I did research. Fascinating, intelligent, and learned, the archivists at most Catholic institutions have been as valuable a resource as the materials that lie within their charge.

Tracey Mitrano created this selection especially for this volume. She used various Catholic Church archives and collections in her research on Catholic higher education for women in New York State. She is completing her doctorate at the State University of New York at Binghamton.

invaluable in locating privately held material.

With all of the documents suggested here, one could write a respectable study of nearby education. There are many more sources available, however, sources that provide access to questions not approachable through the historian's traditional sources. Reflect for a moment about the sources of evidence discussed thus far. Where did they come from? Whose voices does one hear in them?

It is the answers to questions such as those that attracted many historians to the new social history. They found that the traditional sources could tell an important story, but it was a partial story. Its sources were written and hence largely produced by a special, privileged few—women and (mostly) men in positions of authority who wrote about their thoughts and actions concerning education. It was their voices we have largely heard. From their sources we can write a history primarily about them.

Writing the history of nearby education with these sources can produce the same eerie sense we get when we enter a school building during vacation. It is lifeless and hollow. Here we are, writing about schools, yet we cannot hear the voices of the students. Oddly, we can only dimly hear those of teachers and parents. Administrators, bureaucrats, educational theorists, and publishers, yes. But did they make up the daily life of the classroom? Are they the people who come to mind when we think of our own schooling? Are they the center of the educational enterprise?

Thus, to go beyond the formal, largely political history of nearby education, I will next explain some sources and techniques that begin to allow new voices to be heard, to answer some new questions, and to deepen our understanding of the meaning of nearby education.

Suggested Readings

A full introduction to traditional primary source material can be found in Frank Freidel, ed., "Research Methods and Materials," *Harvard Guide to American History* (Cambridge, Mass.: Belknap Press, 1974), pp. 3-134. For information on a broad range of research issues, consult Jacques Barzun and Henry F. Graff, *The Modern Researcher*, rev. ed. (New York: Harcourt, Brace & World, 1970).

David E. Kyvig and Myron A. Marty provide a detailed discussion of the sorts of documents appropriate to local history in *Nearby History: Exploring the Past around You* (Nashville: American Association for State and Local History, 1982). Rather than discussing the types of documents as I have here and in the following chapter, they deal with published and unpublished documents, oral and visual documents, artifacts, landscapes, and buildings.

For further thoughts on using newspaper morgues and indexes, see Catherine L. Covert, "'Jumbled, Disparate, and Trivial': Problems in the Use of Newspapers as Historical Evidence," *Maryland Historian* 13 (Spring 1981): 47-60.

Some of the data sources discussed here and in the next chapter are amenable to quantitative analysis. Those interested in doing quantitative history should consult a good statistics text as a foundation, followed by a text on quantitative methodology, such as Julian L. Simon, *Basic Research Methods in Social Science* (New York: Random House, 1969). Edward Shorter, *The Historian and the Computer: A Practical Guide* (Englewood Cliffs, N.J.: Prentice-Hall, Inc., 1971) has become dated with the emergence of the personal computer but still has valuable ideas and remains useful for those using a mainframe computer. Its concluding chapter has a series of cautions that apply no matter how the technology advances.

Harley P. Holden, "Student Records: The Harvard Experience," *American Archivist* 30 (October 1976): 461-67, is a valuable introduction to the sorts of student records available in many repositories. Although his focus is on higher education, and Harvard University specifically, researchers interested in any aspect of the history of local education as it affects students will profit from reading the article.

The books cited by Jeffrey Mirel in his contribution, "Using Depression Era Youth Studies for Nearby Educational History," are L.A. Menefee and M.M. Chambers, *American Youth: An Annotated Bibliography* (Washington, D.C.: American Council on Education, 1938); Howard Bell, *Youth Tell Their Story* (Washington, D.C.: American Council on Education, 1938); and Ray Johns, *En Route to Maturity* (Detroit: Detroit Board of Education, 1938).

·5·

Listening for Other Voices

MANY OF THE WRITTEN SOURCES FOR THE HISTORY OF local education were created by, and largely for, a small and select group, an elite—college presidents, school boards, state superintendents, local editors, wealthy benefactors. As such, the sources offer a clear view of the actions and thoughts of that elite, but they reveal little about the actions and thoughts of the rest of us. Those sources provide windows on big events but neglect the everyday life of teachers and students. They expose the intentions and perceptions of those in power but obscure, perhaps even distort, the aspirations and values of those using, or used by, educational institutions. Thus, the traditional sources answer many of the questions we have posed, but many more questions, often the most fascinating, cannot be approached adequately with the sources discussed so far.

How can we begin to hear the voices of other people? More specifically, how can we begin to hear what others thought or said about schooling? The great majority of people do not write much about the schools they attended or the education they gained. Students might gripe about a teacher or express their dread about the end of summer vacation; parents might boast about their children's grades. But such comments, if they were recorded at all, are only a fraction of the total written record people left and may not provide a very accurate reflection of the meaning education had for them.

One approach is to use a source such as the ethnic, labor, and minor party presses, discussed in Chapter 4. Those papers tell us much about the thinking and action of the rest of us. If we want to know what immigrant groups, workers, farmers, and other folk were thinking and reading about schooling, we will gain little from most traditional sources. While the men and women who wrote such sources thought they knew what was best for other people, it is not surprising to learn that they were frequently out of touch with the values and aspirations of groups "below" them on the social scale. The ethnic, labor, and political presses provide a starting place in the search for other voices. With what sorts of views of education's value would readers of a Yiddish paper in Brooklyn be familiar? How did the editor of a German foreign-language paper in southern Minnesota respond to anti-German curricula developed for the public schools during the First World War? Did workers in Chicago see the movement toward vocational education in the schools in the 1900s as an attack on craft traditions? What did the farmers of Kansas perceive as the purpose of public higher education? We can approach questions such as these through newspapers, which long ago went out of business.

While those sorts of papers are valuable, they are not nearly enough. They flourished for only a few decades and only where there were enough trade unionists, immigrants, or people active in a political movement to support them. At other times, for other groups, they are not much help. As a result of that problem and others that have left many people historically "inarticulate," social historians have developed strategies that exploit less traditional sources, allowing glimpses of the lives of ordinary people. Even though most folk left no direct historical records in the forms of letters, diaries, essays, or newspaper stories about their exploits, they nonetheless left clear traces of their lives. They were enumerated in censuses and directories; they paid taxes; they worked; they enrolled in schools; they joined organizations; they appeared in photographs; they chose certain kinds of symbols and bought certain kinds of products. You can use those facts and more to learn many fascinating things about how people lived their daily lives.

Compiled Records

For many years genealogists and family historians have used documents compiled by governmental agencies or corporate groups. Historians were slow to see the value of compiled records. The concern to hear the voices of other people, however, alerted social historians to the possibilities in such records, and today some of the most innovative history is being written based on the findings from compiled records.

If any particular source stands out among the compiled documents, it is the census. These remarkable records have enumerated every man, woman, and child in the nation, at least theoretically, at regular intervals since 1790. The federal census began then and has been taken every decade since. Many states and some cities have taken censuses of their own, usually five years after the federal census.

The first few censuses were narrowly focused head-counts. After 1850, however, questions on an increasing range of economic and social issues were included in the enumeration, affording a much fuller picture of American life. Summaries of the painstakingly collected information are published in the *Federal Census of Population, Agriculture and Manufacturing*.

For local historians the manuscript records from the census enumerations are more valuable than the published census. These are the handwritten forms filled out by the census takers and available today on microfilm and, in some places for certain decades, in original manuscript. To protect privacy, manuscript forms are closed for seventy-two years by the federal government. Thus, we have access to all decades up through 1910 (except for the 1890 census, which was lost to fire). State censuses were taken into the 1920s in some states and are available without restrictions.

These manuscript returns permit us to catch glimpses of our community at frequent intervals and learn about ethnic heritage, economy, family size, education, growth, and change. They allow us to locate individuals and families and to trace occupations, employment patterns, educational background, literacy, dates of birth, ethnicity, and value of personal property. They furnish a view of neighborhoods to determine social class, ethnic background or race, and social mobility.

The manuscript census returns for a community or county are a powerful source, capable of exposing much about the extent and effectiveness of schooling for the people of the locality. The returns provide, for instance, an estimate of trends in literacy from the 1850s to 1910, for they indicate the number of individuals over twenty years of age noted as illiterate in each decade's enumeration. Through the returns, you can measure the effectiveness of compulsory school laws by counting the number of children who attended school in the year of the census. With a bit more work, you can establish the relationship of social class, race, ethnicity, or gender to questions of literacy or school attendance.

The possibilities multiply when you add other sources to the information available in the census. If you have found reliable school enrollment records for an extended period of time before 1910, for example, you can link the names in the school records with their parents in the census and ask more precise questions. Were there differences in school attendance patterns by race, ethnicity, or social class? From evidence of social mobility over time, which groups seem to have gained most from educational opportunities? Which had the greatest effect on school attendance—father's occupation, social class, or ethnic background?

No extant school records? Watch the newspaper for lists of public school graduates (before the turn of the century, many papers ran lists of eighth-grade graduates; high school graduation was then a luxury gained by few). Link those names with the names in the census, and determine how common it was to have completed school.

Used with maps, the census returns help establish the contours of neighborhoods and ghettos. Then you can plot the placement of school district boundaries, the location of schoolhouses, and quality of facilities to see whether school boards appeared to respond to class, race, or ethnicity in their decisions.

Tracing Students through Directories and the Census

The historian of nearby education is in a unique position to use sources such as manuscript census returns, city directories, vital records, and school enrollment records innovatively. Linking them allows whole new ranges of questions to be posed, particularly questions of race, gender, family background, and social mobility. We can find out who was most likely to become a teacher, what became of them, who attended what sorts of schools, for how long, and, at least by inference, why.

In the course of research in clerical work and the development of clerical education, Lisa Fine traced several students through the Chicago city directories and the 1880 census. Although, as she notes, these students cannot be considered a representative sample, we can see from this brief essay how these sources give life to early female students in the nineteenth-century business college.

During the last three decades of the nineteenth century, the private business college provided the initial opportunity for women to train for new clerical positions. These profit-oriented schools took advantage of both the desires of women in search of a marketable skill and the business community's search for trained workers in expanding clerical occupations. These first female business college students usually appear only as statistics in the historical record. In the late nineteenth century, however, the Bryant and Stratton Business College of Chicago highlighted the names of its students in the city directory. This advertising technique has allowed me to glimpse the life of these women heretofore lost to the historical record.

Seven out of the thirty-nine female students listed in the 1880 Directory were located in the manuscript census of 1880. They are not a representative sample; rather, their stories serve as examples.

Each of the seven women was single and lived in a family as a daughter or sister of the head of the household. Of the three who had started working at the time of the census, two were shorthand reporters and one was a typist. Six of the seven women were between the ages of sixteen and nineteen. The one woman who was considerably older than that, forty-two years of age, was also the only woman who was not a daughter to the head of household. Anna Mitchell lived with her brother, his wife, and their married son.

Even though most of these women came from middle-class families of craftsmen and small-scale merchants and traders, the families were not all in the same economic condition. Anna Mitchell's brother, for example, was a corn merchant. In addition to the family members described above, the household included two servants. Edith Wignall's family included her father, an editor of a local newspaper, his wife, a young brother, and an Irish servant. Sixteen-year-old Minnie Drechsler, however, lived with her widowed German mother, who kept two Prussian boarders in their home. And Lottie Dalton, a seventeen-year-old typist, lived with a disabled father, a mother and sister, who kept house, and a twenty-five-year-old sister, who was a teacher.

Economic misfortune, then, may have driven some women to business college, but it was certainly not the only reason that women went. Anna Mitchell's work history is illustrative. In 1878, Mitchell was a clerk, but the next year she worked as a teacher. Then in 1880, Mitchell attended business college, and three years later she procured work as a stenographer. Since the household employed two servants, it is unlikely that Mitchell was driven to work out of economic need; rather, her decision to attend business college appears to have been a way to train for a better job. For these women, at least, the way to get a better job was to train in a private business college to become stenographers or typists.

Lisa Fine, an assistant professor at Michigan State University, prepared this essay especially for this volume. The data come from her dissertation, "'The Record Keepers of Property': The Making of a Female Clerical Labor Force in Chicago, 1870-1930," 1985, University of Wisconsin-Madison.

City directories supplement census returns nicely, or they may be used in lieu of census records for periods after 1910 if linked to other records. Issued frequently, these directories give names, addresses, and occupations of most city residents. They are helpful in tracing students or ascertaining the occupational statuses of parents. Although the directories lack much of the information available in the census returns and are not fully reliable for lower-class and migrant people, they do provide information on occupation, geographic and social mobility, and social class, at least indirectly.

We discussed school records in the last chapter as a source that provides answers to traditional questions. These records are valuable, too, as compiled records that give us access to the experiences of common people. As suggested above, school records yield significant data when linked to the census records. But even used alone, they sharpen insight into the lives of students and clarify issues of access and opportunity. These records vary greatly from state to state and from decade to decade in terms of the information elicited from teachers and administrators (and those who filled out the forms were not always conscientious about answering many of the questions that seemed of peripheral importance to the task of education). Not infrequently they include the race or ethnicity of each child and the tax status of the parents. Invariably they indicate gender of the students.

With materials such as these, we can clarify issues of gender and education—who stayed in school longer or attended more regularly, boys or girls? Did the pattern change, and if so when and in what ways? Were there differences in gender experience according to race, ethnicity, or class? We must pose similar important questions for race and education, social class and education, and ethnicity and education.

Vital records are not frequently consulted by historians of education. Vital records are documents each locality keeps on births, marriages, and deaths. Their use for our purposes tend to be specialized, but they are worth keeping in mind. You may use the records to check the accuracy of local school censuses (which I have found often undercount significantly); to ascertain the death rate for school-age children; or to trace teachers who married and changed their names.

In some special situations, a researcher might also be able to use election returns to listen more acutely to the voices of the past, especially the voices of parents and other adults articulating their concerns about education. Before the advent of the secret ballot, the results of some town meetings included roll-call votes of participants. By identifying demographic characteristics of groups of voters through the census and other documents (How old were their children? What was their occupation and social status? What was their age? Their wealth?), we may be able to see patterns in the vote. Michael Katz used that technique tellingly when analyzing a Beverly, Massachusetts, vote that removed the public high school from tax support. He found that skilled craftsmen, facing prolonged economic decline and hardship and knowing that only the children of the more affluent would be able to take advantage of secondary schooling paid for by all taxpayers, voted to abolish the high school.

Such issues are harder to deal with in the era of the secret ballot, but you can borrow techniques from the political scientists to approximate voting patterns roughly. You can learn, for instance, how various precincts voted on educational issues in larger towns and cities. Using census tract information or data compiled from the manuscript census or other sources, you can determine the sorts of variables—average age of voters in each precinct, their economic status, the average size of their families, their educational background, and so forth—that might have affected the vote.

It is worth noting here that as we use these newer materials and the quantitative techniques necessary to exploit them, it is not enough simply to report the results of our calculations. The finality of numbers at times seduces us into thinking so. It may seem adequate to announce, "The areas of the county that voted against the school budget throughout the 1950s averaged 53.7 years of age, with 0.7 children living at home, while those voting for the budget were an average of 18.6 years younger with intact family size of 2.8 children," or to assert, "While men dominated teaching in 1820 in Syracuse, making up over ninety percent of teachers in that decade, they composed only thirty-seven percent in 1890 and less than ten percent of the elementary teachers." Such data are only raw facts, much like the traditional sources that claim a particular starting date for a school or a shift in curriculum between two dates. The facts available from any source require explanation and interpretation. Older and childless couples have not always opposed schooling; what does the phenomenon noted above, then, say about the public perception of the purposes of schooling, today and in the past? The nineteenth-century feminization of teaching took place in a larger historical context; what was it, and what were the consequences?

The work involved in using compiled records might seem onerous or intimidating. Sifting through thousands of names in manuscript census forms, trying to link perhaps several hundred students to their families, or counting live births over four decades and comparing them with enrollments in the same four decades, to say nothing about the quantitative techniques needed to master the material—the notion is numbing.

It need not be, however. In the first place, this is your project. Don't be bullied. Take from this book only what you are comfortable with, and go construct good history. But in the second place, what I have suggested here is not as difficult as it may sound. Perfectly splendid accounts can be crafted with no greater quantitative skills than the ability to count and figure simple percentages. As for the anticipatory dread of doing the linking and counting, just recall that that, too, is a big part of the detective work. The anxiety that many researchers experience when they are new to these sources and techniques has more to do with learning where to find them and how to use them than with the task of working with the material.

Oral Records

It is curious that for ages society's historical memory has been preserved through oral traditions, yet in modern societies oral testimony, the memory of living people, is generally shunned by historians. They prefer written memories, things said in print or handwriting, to the verbal reminiscences of people who lived the events historians are interested in. There are exceptions, naturally. Diplomatic historians are not reluctant to question elder statesmen; political historians flock to interviews with former presidents or congressmen; and cultural historians might seek a seance with a prominent artist. But such practice is limited and reaches virtually only the most noted or noteworthy.

In recent years, however, historians, folklorists, and others have expanded that limited practice. They have realized the vast store of knowledge that would never be written down, that would disappear with the deaths of men and women of all walks of life. Perhaps we have been propelled in part by the fact that modern life discourages our handing on very much evidence of our lives, at least as compared to the recent past. The telephone has replaced letter writing, consumable leisure has replaced reflective activities such as diary or journal writing, and electronic media are crowding out the written word. As a result, the oral history interview is becoming a significant source of evidence in historical writing. For the nearby historian, it can be a major source.

You can gain access to oral history in two ways. First, it is possible that

Hearing the Past through Oral History

Oral history holds great promise as a way to gain information and a perspective on the past. If the scope of study includes the decades after World War I, we may find teachers, students, administrators, or others who remember much that has not survived in print or who have opinions that differ from the extant material.

The excerpt below, from a twenty-three-page transcript, indicates a few of the issues to raise in an oral history interview and the rich insights the process offers. The interviewee was a retired Pittsburgh public school teacher who had taught elementary school for thirty-eight years without a break or a sabbatical. Early in the interview, the interviewer asked questions about her own education, ethnicity, family, parents' occupations, and so forth. He then turned to questions about her experiences as a teacher.

Q: You stated that you had started [teaching] in the 1930s. Do you recall any specific teaching experiences from the 1930s with the Great Depression going on?
A: It was the nicest teaching days of my life because nobody bothered you. You were allowed to teach as you saw fit to teach. No supervisors, no nothing.
Q: So there was no administrative interference? Is that what you are saying?
A: Oh, and another thing, we had to help feed the children — we did a good job of feeding the children.
Q: Did the school district subsidize that or did you?
A: We paid ourselves.
Q: So you are saying that you and other teachers, out of your pockets, paid?
A: Paid. We also took a ten percent cut in our salary.
Q: What was your starting salary, if I may ask?
A: A hundred and thirty a month. . . .
Q: What do you recall about your colleagues, any specific incidences? Were the teachers close, or . . . ?
A: Very close, and very, very dedicated.
Q: What about their general background, preparation for teaching? Similar to yours, more or less?
A: Similar, similar.
Q: Males, females?
A: Up until World War II, it was all females except the gym and woodworking teachers being there.

Q: Were they mostly single or married?

A: *The females had to be single till 1937.*

Q: Why did they have to be single?

A: *The law.*

Q: Was this a state law that mandated it?

A: *A state law. Once you married you had to leave teaching, but there were some married undercover.*

Q: Oh, really. Can you tell me about any of those?

A: *A girlfriend of mine, she went on teaching about two years without them knowing. And there were one or two others that I suspected that . . . they were pretty shrewd about covering it up. . . .*

Q: Did any of the teachers paddle any of the students?

A: *No, all of the thirty-six years of my life I never put a hand on a child.*

Q: What about the other teachers?

A: *No, it was a well-organized, well-run school. That's why I stayed there all those years. . . .*

Q: What do you recall about the salary and the benefits in the 1940s?

A: *We started at $130 if you had a degree. If you didn't have a degree, you started at $120. For a degree, they gave you ten dollars more a month. If you were just a Normal School teacher, then, you know, by the 1940s you had to have a degree before you were hired; that changed. Uh, 1940s. . . 1937 the law passed in Pennsylvania . . . that very important law they are always talking about. . . .*

Q: Tenure?

A: *Tenure was passed in 1937 under Governor Earle.*

Q: So, up to that point, Pittsburgh School teachers had no tenure?

A: *No tenure, no nothing.*

Q: So they could be hired or fired at will, for anything?

A: *Well, the big cities at that time were more liberal in their views than the small towns. The small towns around Pittsburgh, one, for instance: McKees Rocks. When the Republicans got in all the Democratic teachers lost their jobs. When the Democrats got in, all the Republican teachers lost their jobs. So the teachers, I was one of them, we were very militant? Is that the word? We went to meeting after meeting and talk, talk, talk, and we had notable people at our meetings and, finally, tenure was passed under Governor Earle.*

Q: Who sponsored these meetings? Who thought of holding these meetings? Who organized them?

A: *Prominent people from the neighborhood like priests, preachers, even politicians, you know, that knew that it was wrong to allow politics to invade the schools the way they were doing.*

Q: So you imply, then, that there was a great deal of support by a lot of different people for the teachers having tenure?

A: It was immense, immense.

Q: Why?

A: Because. . . in mostly small towns you weren't hired for what you knew, but if you knew the right man at the right time, you became a teacher. You have to remember up till about the 1950s the number one job for a woman in the country was teaching.

Richard J. Altenbaugh, "Margaret Interview," from his Public School Teachers Oral History Project. Altenbaugh has used his extensive collection of oral history interviews in a number of papers and is working on a book on the history of teaching that will use the interviews as a central source.

a nearby college, library, or historical society has begun oral history archives that include reminiscences about nearby teachers, students, or institutions. Many of the items may have been transcribed, making your task of assimilating and evaluating the spoken word a good deal easier.

Second, you can "do" some oral history yourself. If your research includes the last six or seven decades, it is probable that there are people nearby who can answer many of your questions. What better source than one that can respond directly to you?

There are some common-sense, important rules to observe when conducting oral history interviews to assure the fullest possible cooperation. Obviously you must make arrangements with your interviewee well in advance. Be direct. Tell her or him exactly what you are working on, the general sorts of information you will ask about, and how you are going to conduct the interview. Generally it is preferable to interview people in their homes or other places where they are comfortable.

Once you have arranged an appointment, prepare yourself well. Write out your questions beforehand, and have them with you. It may not be necessary or even possible to ask all of them or to pursue them in exactly the order you intended. Be flexible enough to follow up on issues raised in the course of the interview. You should hope that the interview remains relaxed and spontaneous. If it does, it will tend to ramble a bit. But do not, on the other hand, trust that a completely spontaneous, unplanned interview will uncover the information you seek. It may well end up embarrassing both you and your interviewee if you are not prepared to lead the interview.

If at all possible, use a good quality tape recorder. It is extremely difficult to take accurate notes in an interview, and note-taking may distract your subject. Many people are self-conscious around a microphone at first, but most will become accustomed to it. If you have access to a recorder with a built-in microphone, you have won part of the battle. Know how to operate the recorder, and test recording levels before arriving for your appointment.

The oral history interview is most valuable if you transcribe the audio tape. Do this as soon as possible after the interview. Even under the best of conditions (and we seldom have the luxury of good conditions in an oral history interview), portions of an informal conversation are difficult to understand on tape. If the conversation is still fresh in your own memory, you will be better able to reconstruct muffled or indistinct parts of the interview.

You may gain further ideas and tips by dipping into some of the books and articles now available on oral history. The notes to this chapter include many of those I have found worthwhile.

Oral history contributes vital documentation. With carefully planned questions, you uncover facts, ideas, values, and concerns that are not available in any written form, and you gather them from people who would be unlikely to commit them to paper. You literally hear other voices through oral history.

Visual and Material Documents

By adding compiled records and oral history to our tool box, we have expanded considerably the range of information available as we prepare to construct a history of nearby education. We are still limited, though, to articulated traces of past lives. We have reason to be uncomfortable with the notion that the only things of value in our lives, the only things that give our lives meaning, are those that can be written about, spoken, or reduced to check marks on official forms. We should be no less comfortable in limiting our investigation of the past to articulated documents.

We leave all sorts of nonverbal traces behind us. Much of what we know of the past and present and the way we think about the future comes from visual, not verbal, images. Photographs, drawings, displays, paintings, sculpture, architecture, patterns of action, and symbols teach us as surely as written and spoken words.

When I think of the 1920s, for example, I have many images of what that period must have been like, although I did not live through it. Some of those images were constructed, doubtlessly, from things I have read and heard about that period, but many more arise from countless pictures, old movies, fashions in clothing and buildings, and styles of artistic expression dating from the so-called Roaring Twenties (my impressions may be error-ridden, of course, but that is an issue we will take up in the final chapter). I have "read" the visual and material documents from that era, unconsciously for the most part, and have gained insight into the era from them as surely as I did when I read its written documents.

Historians have been reluctant to use visual and material documents. It is true that history texts are crammed with photographs and other visual illustrations, but I am not speaking here of using such documents as illustrations. Rather, I am suggesting that we use photographs, paintings and drawings, iconography, architecture, and the patterns within them as evidence, just as we use written documents. Four types of these documents commend themselves to historians of nearby education: pictures, particularly photographs; items from education's material culture; education's iconography; and buildings.

In the last century and a half, two inventions have vastly expanded the availability of pictures—the lithograph, which made the mass production of drawings and engravings cheap and easy, and the camera, which made possible initially the precise two-dimensional reproduction of relatively still scenes by experts and eventually the even more precise and instantaneous capturing of virtually any scene by virtually anyone. Both inventions provide the historian of nearby education with a wealth of visual images of campuses, schoolhouses, teachers, students, school activities, and the communities in which the school was embedded. We need merely to learn how to ask significant questions of those images, just as we do of traditional written documents.

The most obvious question is: What is pictured? What can we ascertain about the subject from the obvious detail? If it is a class portrait, how are the students arranged? Why? For example, are they lined up rigidly, facing the camera? Engaged in school work? Dressed formally or in everyday attire? I am confident that part of my image of the 1920s comes from class photographs of college students, lounging, leaning, and standing in whimsical, studied poses.

If the subject is an exterior view of a school building, what can we determine about its location, maintenance, and style? If we have a good selection of "formal" school pictures from the institution we are working with, we can watch for their focus. Does the focus change over the years? What is included in the photographs? What is excluded? What might be seen in them that the photographer might not even have been aware of? What do the photographs suggest as being most important to record? Do we find, for instance, more concern with the formal facade of the local elementary school than with the playground, the area most memorable to the students? Do photographs from the college archives shift over time from showing campus social life to academic pursuits?

Beyond the obvious questions, a major consideration when evaluating pictures is perspective or point of view of the photographer or the artist. How is the picture framed? What is included? What is excluded? Crucially, how did the photographer wish to present this moment in time to him- or herself and the audience? Remember that pictures, even snapshots, are not random slices of reality, not images of "things as they really were." Pictures are affected by conventions of the society. They are efforts to capture a reality as interpreted by the person taking the picture. They focus on what that person perceives as important; they reflect an effort, often unconscious, to represent, or re-present, reality to viewers in ways the artist or photographer assumes will be meaningful.

To illustrate this point, imagine a relatively simple mobile robot, capable of managing stairs, doors, and busy streets, but little more. Imagine, further, that I have fixed this robot with a camera on a rotating arm and set the camera to take a snapshot every ninety seconds. What would we have after several days of our robot's wandering about a school or a town, randomly snapping photos? Mostly, meaningless shots of stair rails, doorknobs, blank walls, blurred automobiles, uninteresting vistas, and other ill-composed, insignificant pictures. We would certainly have accurate images of whatever the robot passed by, but we would not have photos that we would find meaningful or significant. Why? Because there was no one behind the lens snapping the pictures when the image in the view finder fit the photographer's perceptions of appropriate, meaningful data to communicate to an audience.

Or, put another way, we have come to expect a picture to portray a significant reality. We expect the photographer to portray us to ourselves in ways that we recognize and accept. As Thomas Schlereth said of snapshots and family albums, "Their research value probably lies not in their proclivity to detail life as it is, but in their tendency to express communal ideals, beliefs, and attitudes. On an immediate level, they seem to represent shared notions

Like verbal sources, photographs provide data for the historian of nearby education. These two photographs, for instance, inform us about two athletic opportunities for students in small high schools in west central Minnesota in 1912 and 1920. They tell us more, however, about experience, values, and expectations if we observe the placement of people and things, the stances, postures, gestures, and expressions. What do these two pictures imply about male and female athletes in the second decade of the twentieth century?

of appropriate moments to photograph." We photograph what we want to remember; hence, the photograph is a "stylized reality."

Knowing this is central to the task of using pictures in historical research, for then we can seek to understand what the photographer saw as significant, real, recognizable, and thus worthy of remembering. If we find many pictures containing the same pictorial elements, we may hypothesize that others accepted their significance, reality, and recognizability. They, in turn, adopted the conventions or honored the pictures by saving or publishing them.

Those reflections, then, suggest a series of further questions to ask of pictorial evidence. How was the picture intended to present reality? How did the photographer hope to portray this activity, or this group, to the viewer? What do the conventions of the portrayal say about the assumptions and values of the artist and the audience? What, out of the total reality of the moment, did the photographer choose to make memorable?

Using photographs as documents, not merely as illustrations of conclusions drawn from other documents, opens up the possibility of using plentiful but neglected sources. Educational institutions that had active journalism departments are likely to have bulging files of photographs of school activities. The local newspaper may also have a photograph morgue with pictures from the college or school. Almost universally, furthermore, secondary schools, academies, colleges, and other institutions serving adolescents and adults have published yearbooks for several decades.

How can one use yearbooks in historical research? Are they not primarily individual pictures of students, the seniors in formal wear, the underclasspeople in appropriately less sophisticated garb?

They are that, often, but they are also much more. You can use them effectively by comparing them over time and by "reading" the data in each one. If, as argued, photographs reflect shared values, ways of representing ourselves to ourselves, you can begin by simply asking: What is pictured? What is not? By way of illustration, I think it interesting that most yearbooks from the last four decades or more portray a great variety of campus activities—but hardly any learning, study, or inquiry. Significantly, when I ask my students what they *remember* about secondary school, they confirm that, *for students*, secondary school is about all sorts of fun things but seldom about the joy of learning. The yearbooks portray a shared reality if you learn how to read it.

Here a comparison over time may be valuable. Yearbooks from the early years of the century have a markedly greater academic bent than do those from more recent years. If we find that pattern in our research, we might ask when the shift away from student concern with academics took place? Why? What replaced the concern with academics?

Yearbook pictures yield other data. As Nancy Green suggested in the illustration in Chapter 2, researchers learn much about who participated in what extracurricular activities and how those changed over time. The status hierarchy of activities may often be inferred from visual evidence in the yearbooks. Yearbooks indicate the race of students and teachers, information that may not be available elsewhere. Used with other sources that indicate social class, yearbooks enrich our understanding of which groups most effectively used the school and in what ways.

Another form of historical document is material culture, the name given to the *things* people have left behind. Like other nonverbal sources, material culture adds to knowledge, but we must learn how to "read" it.

Because of the nature of the enterprise, perhaps, many of the artifacts of nearby education are written documents, textbooks, students' assignments, and so forth, and as such are not what come to mind when we speak of material culture. What is part of education's material culture? Among other things, think of the trophy cases that stand prominently in the halls of secondary schools and academies. Their very prominence speaks volumes on the priorities of many schools. Their contents document the prowess of athletic teams, but that may be ascertained more completely and more accurately with other sources. But look again. Most cases I have examined contained more than athletic trophies. What other endeavors are celebrated there? Are there awards, for instance, from civic organizations or others outside the institution? What do they say about the relationship between the school and the community? Check the walls of principals' and deans' offices for similar awards.

In the older halls of colleges, we may also find the precursor of the college's science laboratories, the "scientific cabinets" filled with curiosities. Other "learning aides" may show up in closets and attics or in museums that have collected school artifacts. The electronic educational technology of the 1980s has a long and uninspired pedigree of gadgets and devices intended to make teaching more efficient or learning less problematical. They are all worthy of critical attention. The school bell, teachers' desk bells, flagpoles and room flags, quills and inkwells, freshmen's beanies, school mascots and insignia, and playground equipment and school toys make up other physical evidence of the experience of education in the past.

Material culture helps us describe the past more precisely, to find patterns and to locate discontinuities. On one level, we may analyze the artifact to determine how it was used, what it was like to have used it, and when it was used. How rapidly and with how much facility could a child write with a hand-sharpened pen, and what effect might the experience have had on his or her desire to write in nineteenth-century schools? Who encouraged the use of learning aids and audio-visual materials? What was the response of teachers to these devices? When did flags and patriotic ceremonies become ubiquitous parts of public schooling?

As we study the artifacts of education, however, we need to go beyond their functional significance to attempt to determine their symbolic significance. The antiquated chemistry laboratory, for example, allowed students to replicate the chemical reactions they read about. But the lab also symbolized an allegiance to a new mode of learning—learning by doing—and to a modern, scientific age, in which increasingly the scientists and their paraphernalia became dominant cultural symbols. It takes little imagination to understand the symbolism of the paintings of Washington and Lincoln that hung in most schoolrooms. But what is symbolized by their disappearance? When did that happen, and why? What replaced them? What does that symbolize?

School buildings and educational iconography are artifacts, too. But because of their value, and their neglect by historians, I am treating them separately here to emphasize them. I know of no printed material on interpreting the iconography of education and little on the significance of educational architecture, so we have nothing to go on but my own thoughts and the evidence I have from my own efforts to break some new ground.

What, first, is meant by educational iconography? Icons are images intended to convey an idea or evoke a response, as when religious icons are used to promote piety. Educational iconography, then, refers to the conscious use of symbolic representation of educational ideas or themes, and the analysis and interpretation of educational iconography involves locating and attempting to understand the images and the ideas to which they refer.

We can describe the symbols found on and in college and school buildings, but how can we interpert them? We begin from the assumption that overt symbols and architectural styles reflect social values. We add to that the assertion that changes in symbolic imagery and architectural style reflect changes in values and outlook. And, recalling that schooling is a relatively conscious process of passing on the culture, values, and outlook of the society to the next generation, we assume that overt symbolism on school buildings is likewise intended to pass on certain accepted notions of the meaning and use of formal education. They are, in other words, designed with one eye toward the "lessons" someone wants to impart to young people.

Thus it is important to be aware of the bas-reliefs, engravings, sculptures, paintings, and other ornamentation designed into schoolhouses. These sorts of details, even more than styles of architecture, were chosen with conscious educational intent. Those who chose the icons and those who approved of them in the plans sought through those icons to foster certain ideas or attitudes about the schooling process to the young people attending lessons in that building. If we pay attention to the detail, we can often divine their intent and learn much about assumptions concerning the purposes and ends of education.

Interpreting the iconography of nearby schools.

The sculptures and bas-reliefs pictured here are found on two school buildings in Binghamton, New York. The first two are from a building constructed during the first decade of the twentieth century, while the remainder come from an early 1930s school building. In each case, the ornamentation was intended to convey a particular conception of education to the young people who used these buildings and the public who supported education. What may we conclude about early twentieth-century Binghamtonian notions of the ends of education? How had those notions changed by 1931? What became of the view of youth over those years? Can we make any generalizations about the probable curricular emphasis in each era?

Some school buildings are rich in iconography; others have nothing beyond the oblique statement of the building design itself. Interior objects, especially murals, are more common than exterior icons. Educational buildings constructed within the last two decades seem particularly devoid of educational ornamentation. But before you assume that the schools near you have none, go take a second look. The lamp of learning in graceful bas-relief stands prominently above the main door to the middle-school near me, built originally as the district high school. Flanking it are representations of the two hemispheres, while topping the Greek pillars are two other bas-reliefs of men reclining against the wheels of industry and sheaves of grain. I have talked to students and teachers who have entered that building often without once noticing the fascinating detail around them.

One could use that fact to argue that an analysis and interpretation of the iconography is fallacious as evidence of the history of nearby education. As students, we paid no attention to the messages someone intended to give us. They had no effect.

My point is not that educational icons necessarily *did* convey the cultural messages someone intended for them to convey. I am unsure how we would ever measure that—it is difficult enough to measure how much of the more explicit classroom message students carry away with them. My point is that it is valuable to know what someone *intended* for students to learn, whether they learned it or not. Anyway, we know enough today about subliminal messages to argue that even if we did not take notice of the Latin motto, the scriptural injunction, the images of quills and scrolls, our ways of thinking and of seeing may have been nonetheless affected in some way.

We can work with educational iconography in two ways. We can first note all the examples we find, ascertaining the dates they were created, and then attempt to explain what their educational intent might have been. Here a good collection of photographs and lithographs of earlier buildings in our area of research will be invaluable. If the scope of our study extends back even a few decades, many buildings we want to study no longer stand. The details on others may have been destroyed in remodelings and expansions. Interior icons are even more susceptible to loss and alteration.

Our work at this first step can be facilitated with traditonal documents. We may find an architect's explanation of the choice of decorative items or a news reporter's interpretation of the icons in an article describing the completion of the building. The students, in their first blush of pride in their new surroundings, may have noticed and explained to themselves, in their newspaper, literary magazine, or yearbook, the meaning of symbols in the building.

Second, note the changes in the form and content of the iconography over time. What themes emerge as others disappear? Do any reappear? Are different messages intended for younger children than for high school or college students? What is implied about the nature of learning, the purposes of schooling, or the ends of education? How do those implications change over time, and why?

The school buildings themselves are documents and forms of iconography. Be aware of the location of schools. Why were they built where they were? Are there consistent patterns to the siting of new schools? What does the physical evidence suggest about quality of construction and patterns of maintenance in various neighborhoods? Were some neighborhoods favored at the expense of others? Who benefited? Who lost? As you ask these questions, be sensitive to the changing racial and class characteristics of neighborhoods.

Study the architectural styles of the buildings as well. If changing styles suggest changing values and outlooks, what do the changes in a college's architectural plans reflect? Were the changes in the style of public schoolhouses in your town due solely to technical changes in construction, or do they also reflect deeper changes in perceptions of youth and education? Were there differences in the styles of buildings provided for different groups of students? Who got which kinds, and what might the students have learned about their place in the society from the sorts of structures they entered daily? Is there educational significance, for example, in the fact that a prestigious college near me boasts quiet, tree-lined streets, stately academic buildings, and ivy-covered libraries, while ten miles away a two-year college specializing in vocational preparation is housed in a single building that, from any perspective, looks like an electronics assembly plant?

Be concerned not only with exterior details, as the architectural historian might be, but also with interiors. What have classrooms been like in the past? What may one learn about schooling from their arrangement? How did teachers or administrators organize and use space? Did the arrangement of rooms, furnishings, and structures influence relationships among members of the school community? Was there a specific place for boys and girls, for minority pupils, for administrators and teachers? Were there significant

Interpreting the Changing Architecture of Schools in Newark Valley.

The early schools serving the children of Newark Valley, New York, were one- and two-room schoolhouses such as this. These "Greek Temples of Learning" drew their architectural inspiration from the Greek Revival style. Might Greek ideals of learning have been implied?

In the 1890s, the Victorian ideal of domesticity influenced the construction of this village school-house, now the local post office. Its lines recall contemporaneous upper-middle-class homes. Have notions of learning and childhood changed from those suggested earlier in the century?

By 1930, consolidations had made the 1890s building too small, and this structure was built following more formal, rational lines. The building reflects the style of governmental buildings around the nation. Has growing statism affected the orientation of schooling?

A new elementary school was built in the mid 1950s, and the earlier building became the secondary school. Nathan T. Hall Elementary School looks like a modern factory but probably reflects more accurately the decline of overt symbolism and the triumph of cost-accounting architecture. Is there here also a shift in the notion of schooling away from humane concerns and toward technical issues?

The new high-school building stands outside the village looking for all the world like the corporate headquarters of a small but prosperous firm. Built in the early 1970s, it shares with Nathan T. Hall Elementary School the flight from symbolism. What notion of the uses and values of learning are implied? Do the most recent choices of architecture suggest that the classical, humanistic notion of education has shifted to a narrower concern with preparing workers for modern industry?

differences in classrooms serving different clientele? If photographs of older schoolrooms include students and teachers, where were they most often pictured and in what relationship to the educational artifacts and to each other? What can one conclude from those facts? The two colleges mentioned earlier furnish an illustration. The first includes small seminar rooms and private offices for its professors, while the second has crowded classrooms nearly indistinguishable from most high schools, while its professors have only open cubicles, like those found in a modern modular office. What may one conclude about the messages being broadcast to the two student populations about themselves, about learning, and about society?

We are now in a position to hear voices from the past and to begin to construct a history from what those voices have to say. The next chapter speaks to the issues of the actual construction of nearby history.

Suggested Readings

Guidance in the use of manuscript census material may be gained from Robert G. Barrows, "The Manuscript Federal Census: Source for a 'New' Local History," *Indiana Magazine of History* 69 (1973): 181-92; Sam Bass Warner, Jr., "A Local Historian's Guide to Social

Statistics," in *Streetcar Suburbs: The Process of Growth in Boston, 1870-1900* (Cambridge: Harvard University Press, 1962), pp. 169-78; and Lutz Berkner, "The Use and Misuse of Census Data for the Historical Analysis of Family Structure," *Journal of Interdisciplinary History* 4 (1975): 721-38. Frequently the state census asked more questions of interest to historians of education than the federal census did. For information on the state censuses, see Henry J. Dubester, *State Censuses: An Annotated Bibliography*, 1944 (Westport, Conn.: Greenwood Press, 1976).

Michael B. Katz's study, *The Irony of Early School Reform: Educational Innovation in Mid-Nineteenth Century Massachusetts* (Boston: Beacon Press, 1968) uses a number of the sources discussed in this chapter. On the abolition of the Beverly High School, see pp. 19-112, and the data in Appendix D, pp. 272-9. The other appendices to this influential volume indicate other sorts of information that may be gleaned from a variety of sources—industrial surveys, demographic reports, and tax records—seldom used by historians of education.

There is a wealth of material available on oral history techniques. The quarterly journal, *Oral History Review*, is filled with helpful articles on conducting interviews, editing, legal issues, and so forth. Among many other valuable sources, see particularly Willa K. Baum, *Transcribing and Editing Oral History* (Nashville: American Association for State and Local History, 1981); Cullom Davis, Kathryn Back, and Kay McLean, *Oral History: From Tape to Type* (Chicago: American Library Association, 1977); Paul Thompson, *The Voice of the Past: Oral History* (New York: Oxford University Press, 1978); and David K. Dunaway and Willa K. Baum, eds., *Oral History: An Interdisciplinary Anthology* (Nashville: American Association for State and Local History, 1984). Among articles, see William W. Cutler, III, "Oral History—Its Nature and Uses for Educational History," *History of Education Quarterly* 11 (Summer 1971): 184-94. John N. Neuenschwander, *Oral History and the Law* (Denton, Texas: Oral History Association, 1985), a pamphlet available from the association, is required reading.

While there are a number of articles available on photographs as historical evidence, I have found few that are actually helpful for the sorts of purposes I have discussed here. There is an inordinate amount of concern with ascertaining such instrumental issues as the photographer, date, subject, and location, but little concern with interpretive issues. Among the sources that do give some help in interpretation, see Paul Byers, "Cameras Don't Take Pictures," *Columbia University Forum* 9 (Winter 1966): 27-31; F. Jack Hurley, "There's More than Meets the Eye: Looking at Photographs Historically," *Center for Southern Folklore Magazine* 3 (Winter 1981): 6-7; Marsha Peters and Bernard Mergen, "'Doing the Rest': The Use of Photographs in American Studies," *American Quarterly* 29 (1977): 280-303; and Michael Thomason, "The Magic Image Revisited: The Photograph as a Historical Source," *Alabama Review* 31 (April 1978): 83-91. I found the most useful to be Thomas J. Schlereth, "Mirror of the Past: Historical Photography and American History" in *Artifacts and the American Past* (Nashville: American Association for State and Local History, 1980), pp. 11-47; I have quoted in this chapter from pages 42 and 43 of that volume.

If you intend to do extensive work in photographs and other nonverbal documents, spend some time considering the provocative ideas of John Berger. His assertion, "The way we see things is affected by what we know or what we believe," lies at the heart of my comments on the interpretation of pictures and of material culture. See particularly his *Ways of Seeing* (London: British Broadcasting Corp. and Penguin Books, 1972). The quotation above is from page 8.

On the use of artifacts and material culture as historical evidence, you will gain insights from Thomas J. Schlereth, *Artifacts and the American Past* (Nashville: American Association for State and Local History, 1980); Mary Johnson, "What's in a Butterchurn or a Sadiron? Some Thoughts on Using Artifacts in Social History," *Public Historian* 5 (Winter 1983): 61-81; and John T. Schlebecker, "The Use of Objects in Historical Research," *Agricultural History* 51 (January 1977): 200-08. David J. Meltzer, "Ideology and Material Culture," in *Modern Material Culture: The Archeology of Us*, edited by Richard A. Gould and Michael B. Schiffer (New York: Academic Press, 1981), pp. 113-26, provides a thought-provoking perspective lacking in the other essays, while Cary Carson, "Doing History with Material Culture," in *Material Culture and the Study of American Life*, edited by Ian M.G. Quimby (Winterthur, Del.: Winterthur Museum, 1978), pp. 41-64, offers a good corrective to the material culture promoters' more naive enthusiasms.

Some of the comments in those sources are of value also in studying the architecture of schools; see also Lucius F. Ellsworth and Linda V. Ellsworth, "House-Reading: How to Study Historic Houses as Symbols of Society," *History News* 35 (May 1980): 9-13. About the only helpful sources dealing directly with the built environment of schools are Norris Brock Johnson, "The Material Culture of Public School Classrooms: The Symbolic Integration of Local Schools and National Society," *Anthropology and Education Quarterly* 11 (Fall 1980): 173-90; and Norris Brock Johnson, "School Spaces and Architecture: The Social and Cultural Landscape of Educational Environments," *Journal of American Culture* 5 (Winter 1982): 79-88.

·6·

Building the Structure, Clinching the Case

WE HAVE BY NOW SURVEYED THE GROUND, DRAWN UP the plans, located the sources, and gathered the tools. Now we can begin to measure and cut, evaluate and weigh. By the end of this process, we will have constructed a solid history. Or, to continue to mix imagery, now we can scrutinize the clues, ponder the evidence, look for connections and contradictions, on the way to solving our puzzle.

Proper Care of Material

Before moving on, consider how we can best do the routine task of physically gathering and retaining our material. I have seen nearly every imaginable mode of note taking and have no doubt that some are much better than others. Let me share two inviolable rules and a couple of suggestions of a more modest sort.

Rule number one: Keep an absolutely accurate bibliography file. Write out the full bibliographical citation to every source consulted, whether it is a secondary source or a letter in a manuscript collection. Make out a card on the source whether it proves valuable or not. Do not put on this card any of the evidence gleaned from the source. Keep the bibliography file separate from the data.

It is useful to include on the bibliography card a brief note summarizing the contents of the source and an even briefer evaluative comment. Several months from now you may not remember what a book or article has to say. Your summary and evaluation will help you recall it quickly.

Rule number two: Be absolutely accurate with all your sources. Double-check all quotations. If you paraphrase, do it in such a way as to avoid the possibility of later inadvertently using the original wording. In other words, avoid plagiarism. Be sure to include all page references in the note accurately, and remember that you need the page numbers not only for direct quotations but for all information acquired from other writers.

These two rules will save untold trouble later. An incomplete citation will force you to retrace your steps unnecessarily. If the original was a primary source, it may be difficult to relocate it without the full citation. But much worse than the extra work is the problem of purposefully or inadvertently using someone else's words. Plagiarism is to the historian's craft what fraud is to business. It is not merely sloppy work; it is theft.

As for the suggestions: Use a uniform size note card or paper. In graduate school I had a colleague who wrote research notes on whatever happened to come to hand—paper torn out of spiral-bound notebooks, legal-size sheets, half-sheets, note-pad paper. By the time she had completed her work on a particular project, she had an unmanageable pile and was unable to find anything she wanted. When I last saw her writing up her research, she was in the middle of her apartment with the floor, tables, and chairs covered with odd stacks of paper, trying to sort out her data.

Note-size paper or cards are generally preferable to full sheets. It is more efficient, particularly in the writing stage, to have each discrete piece of information on a separate card. The cards can then be quickly sorted and filed by topic. Be sure that every card includes enough bibliographical information to identify its source quickly and the page number or other location of the specific information written on the card. With a separate, complete bibliography file, one can abbreviate the citation on the notes—author's last name, shortened title, and page number will suffice. The larger cards, 4" X 6" or 5" X 8", are better than the 3" X 5" cards, because one can get much more information on each card.

As soon as the research begins, determine the major topic categories. These categories will emerge naturally from the questions you are posing. Then it is a simple matter to indicate at the top of each card the type of information contained on that card and to file it under the appropriate category. Thus, for instance, if a researcher were to study the education of Afro-Americans in a community's public schools, he or she might have file headings for "teachers," with names of teachers, information about how long they taught, race, sex and age; "salaries of teachers," under which is filed information on black and white teachers' salaries; "enrollment data," for comparative figures on white and black school enrollments; "census data," with data on the size of the local black community; and a variety of other categories for information on the white and black communities' perception of the value and purpose of black education, efforts to improve the schooling of black children, and so forth. As the work develops, new categories will suggest themselves. With information categorized topically, a researcher may quickly evaluate the evidence on any particular issue.

If you have a personal computer, try one of the new text data management systems. These allow you to type information directly on a disk file and to retrieve it by any of a number of keywords. Let's say that you have located an Urban League report from the 1940s on nearby black schools. The report has statistical data as well as evaluative comments. By summarizing the relevant data and quoting and paraphrasing the qualitative information in an extended note, you can quickly locate the data from that report on promotion rates of black students, for instance, as well as all other data on the same issue from other sources, through a rapid keyword search. Likewise, for a discussion of clashing opinions on education for minority children in the 1940s, the program will retrieve the relevant material from the Urban League and all other similar material that you have saved.

In one sense, of course, the computer is nothing more than a rather expensive electronic file box. It does little more than one can do with five dollars worth of file cards and a shoe box. Its advantages are that many items you will uncover have information that applies to two, three, and even four different topics. With file cards, you must make a copy for each topic or leave notes for yourself to cross check under other topics. You may avoid that problem by using note paper rather than cards and making as many carbon copies of an item as necessary. Still, the computer simplifies that task. Furthermore, if after gathering the material, you realize that there is a different question that might be posed, the keyword search capability of a good text data management system makes short work of collecting information that you would have to find by a slow perusal of every card in the file. Finally, the computer will save a good deal of typing, since the data are already typed. The data can be electronically moved directly into the text.

Working with the Material

The evidence a researcher accumulates is simply a mass of facts, opinions, quotations, and other bits of data. It is like the pile of lumber, stack of plywood, and bales of insulation carpenters accumulate before they begin to construct a house. In that form it is not yet of use to them. They must evaluate the various pieces, measure, cut, discard the bad pieces, and then put all the pieces together in ways that will form a house. Likewise, the researcher must also evaluate, weigh, cut, and discard portions of his or her evidence and then put the pieces together in a coherent pattern.

Not all evidence is of equal value. Some of it is not true; some is only partially true; some is simply irrelevant. So, just as the detective evaluates the conflicting and partial testimony and clues, we must weigh our evidence. How do we do that? By being skeptical of sources and subjecting evidence

This is the St. Louis School Board in 1903. What does the design of the school board room suggest about how the board functions? Is there space for the public? What about the size of the board? Its gender and race? What does the members' dress suggest? Note the spitoons on the floor.

to careful assessment.

A healthy skepticism of the sources is essential. Bias and distortions of various sorts are likely to be present in any source. We need not lament that; it is inevitable. We need only be aware of the sorts of distortions that might appear, watch for them, take them into account as we analyze the evidence, and, when possible, attempt to correct them by seeking further evidence.

Novice historians frequently expect newspapers to be their most objective source. Inaccuracies abound in print journalism, however, and editorial slant is always present. Even such decisions as where to run a story—on the front page or buried near the classified ads—and how much space to devote to it inevitably reflect values and priorities of publishers and editors. It cannot be otherwise; not every item can make the front page nor achieve equal coverage. But the bias is not simply a matter of layout priorities. The editor who considers the academic training of women a waste of money and a danger to female health will simply not give the local female academy the same coverage given to the men's college across town. Importantly, the editor's bias does not mean you will not use the paper in a study of women's education; the editor's statements made up part of what local people knew about the schooling of females and, hence, may be important data even if the researcher disagrees with the bias.

Other print documents are likely also to be slanted. School publications, such as catalogues and recruitment material, will naturally portray the institution as positively as possible. School newspapers are seldom reliable sources on sensitive issues about faculty or administrators or student discipline problems. School administrators have not been hesitant to censor school papers, even in colleges.

The publications of professional organizations and government agencies must likewise be read with a wary eye. Each has its own interests to promote and its own territory to defend.

There are distortions even in the archives. Those distortions arise in part from the pattern of collecting and preserving material. We are many times more likely to find material from social elites and well-funded agencies than from ordinary people and grass-roots groups. The former tend to be much more aware of their historical significance and to save especially those things that will cast them in the best historical light. Distortions arise also because an atypical citizen, the local hero or activist, for instance, is likely to be overrepresented in some collections. The files of organizations and bureaus will tend to have material written predominantly by individuals with vested interests, strong feelings, or clearer positions on an issue than may be generally true of the population.

City directories and manuscript censuses are not error-free. Directories underrepresented working people and transients, sometimes seriously. Fraud sometimes crept into manuscript census returns, particularly for poorer sections of cities, which some census takers did not care to visit. Some areas were missed completely; others occasionally were estimated or fabricated entirely.

The possibility for error in oral histories springs both from the problems of distortion discussed above, as well as from the fact that the recollections are usually recorded long after the events. Memory is highly selective and prone to lapses and unintended distortion. As important as oral history technique is, it has its limitations. Oral testimony must be subjected to the same rigorous criticism that applies to written testimony.

Finally, material culture, too, is liable to be slanted in ways that we must be aware of if we are to use it effectively and critically. Take photographs, for example. A photographer can do much to "color" or bias a photo, just as an editor slants a news story to fit certain preconceptions. Thus, documentary photographs of crowded—or underused—classrooms may have been posed in a particular way or taken at a particular moment to emphasize the need for new classrooms—or for lower educational expenditures.

Historians evaluate their evidence in two ways before they accept it. There is no reason to burden this discussion with the technical jargon that is applied to the process. Essentially, the first form of assessment asks whether the document we are using is authentic while the second asks whether it is true. The first form looks for intentional and accidental errors, plagiarisms, forgeries, and so forth. While we should be alert to those possibilities, they are probably of less concern to us than the second form of evaluation. Not many documents of the sort we will be using are likely to be inauthentic.

It is important to realize that a document may be authentic and still be untrue. A report by a headmaster of an academy might assert that all the pupils in the institution had mastered Latin and trigonometry. We may be certain that the headmaster did, indeed, write the report. And yet, using the second criteria, we may also be certain that the report was false.

Note, furthermore, that although we might prove the report false, we might still remain interested in the report. Its truth or falsity does not necessarily determine its value. The very fact that the headmaster submitted a false

Even play time provides us with information about education. What sorts of questions and ideas can be generated by a photograph such as this one, taken in Shelby County, Iowa, in the 1930s?

report is a valuable piece of historical evidence. But we certainly must be able to know the difference between true and false evidence.

How do we go about weighing the evidence to establish its accuracy? What questions should we ask? How do we "criticize" evidence?

We start by asking if the real meaning of the evidence is different from its literal meaning? Are words used in unusual or archaic ways? Is the statement meant to be ironic? A nineteenth-century document speaking of the number of scholars in the local school does not mean "scholar" in the modern sense of one who devotes his or her whole life to learning, researching, and teaching. Rather, the document is simply using an earlier accepted use of "scholar" to refer to young pupils. An article by a local writer speaking of "the number of excellent folk who are giving their time and thought to this ideal amusement of raising boys" may be praising educational reformers but is more likely being sardonic. Our use of that evidence depends crucially on our understanding of the meaning of the evidence.

We need to ask next how well could the author have observed what he or she is reporting? Was the author in a position to know accurately? What sorts of biases might the observer have? We would have reason to lack confidence in testimony about the low quality of teachers from an absentee landowner who felt taxes were too high.

When did the observer record the observations? Soon after the fact or much later? What was the observer's intention in doing so? For whom? Did the writer, consciously or otherwise, distort or modify the report to fit the desires of the intended audience?

We will never find ideal evidence. To do so would require a neutral, disinterested, objective observer in an ideal position to know all the relevant facts, recording observations in a literal style using modern terminology, and writing immediately after the fact for his or her own use. Without those impossible preconditions, how should we respond to evidence that these questions cast in a dubious light?

In the first place, notice that the evidence will not "flunk" these tests. What these questions do is to help evaluate the evidence. We may still use the statement about teachers from the disgruntled landowner or taxpayer, but we will use it with care, warning readers of the sort of evidence that it is. We will view it in its correct light.

And in the second place, we will seek to amass as much evidence as possible and weigh each piece against the others. We will seek corroborating testimony from the best sources possible. After careful evaluation and analysis, we will come to some judgment about the truth of each piece of evidence. We will use what we judge to be the most truthful to construct our history, and we will reinforce that construction by explaining why that evidence is more valid than contradictory evidence.

How much corroborating evidence is necessary to establish a fact? There are no precise rules here, but A Guide to Historical Method provides a convenient suggestion:

In general, we may say that the corroboration of relatively small events ought to be easier than corroboration of large complex events; that accounts of physical actions are generally easier to feel confident of than descriptions of states of mind; that it is easier to corroborate testimony on commonplace matters than on things people care enough about to lie and to torture their observations; that some matters scarcely can be reliably corroborated, because almost everyone either avoids testimony or feels no obligation to tell the truth (e.g., crime, espionage, illicit sexual activity, treason).

There are times, of course, when no corroborating evidence is forthcoming. I once learned from a single source that a particular school in a county I was investigating had no fixed location. The school served a large, mobile lumber camp, which moved with the logging operation. The schoolhouse was a railroad boxcar fixed up with windows and a stove. As the camp moved deeper into the forest, the crew moved the boxcar down the tracks with the camp, and school continued on a rail spur at the new location. No other source mentioned the boxcar school, and my source of the story had proved on other occasions to be given to a certain amount of self-serving exaggeration. Should I have used the evidence?

I decided to use it and even embellished it a bit with a surmise that a well-built boxcar of that era might have made a schoolhouse that was more snug in the cold months than many of its one-room counterparts. My judgment was based on two considerations. First, although my source had not always proved reliable, he had no particular reason to mislead his audience about this particular fact. Second, the facts were of little consequence to the larger argument I was making in the study. Their inclusion or exclusion would not have altered my conclusions. The story of the boxcar school added some color to the story—nothing more. Those are the sorts of considerations on which our judgments must be based.

After we have subjected our evidence to rigorous criticism and corroboration, have weighed and evaluated it, we begin the process of synthesis and interpretation. This is the step at which we begin to seek patterns in the evidence before us, as the detective attempts to piece together a plausible account of the case. What story emerges most naturally from the evidence? What answers to the many questions posed earlier seem to account for our evidence in the best ways? What alternative explanations can we find? Which alternative seems to have the greatest claim to truth? Are any pieces of evidence left unaccounted for by our explanations? Does any of our evidence contradict our explanation? If the answer to either of the latter two questions is yes, we need to do more research, critique our evidence more rigorously, or think more critically about our synthesis and interpretation, perhaps all three.

This overschematizes the processes one goes through in analyzing evidence and constructing a history. I know of no historian who would gather all data before evaluating them or wait until they were all evaluated before beginning to think about synthesis. Each aspect of the process will proceed in the order suggested here, obviously, but once we have begun one step, we can begin the next step on the material gathered to that point.

In that way, research becomes an organic rather than a mechanical process. Skepticism about a source will make one more critical of other sources and more diligent in the search for more evidence. The facts turned up in one area will suggest new questions. Emerging answers will suggest possible syntheses to be tested and modified with new evidence, further questions, more careful analysis and evaluation.

Finishing and Presenting the Construction

You have searched and researched, questioned and listened. You have measured and evaluated, analyzed and cut. You have pieced your evidence together, interpreting it in light of your understanding of the context and the facts as you can now judge them. You have constructed history.

The process could stop here. You have extended your own memory by your construction of the history of how people have learned or promoted learning in places near you. You have the opportunity, however, to extend the collective memory as well, the memory of the society. Why not share your work with others?

When one considers sharing history, the first thought is usually about books or articles. Printed pages deliver history. If you have done a particularly careful job of researching and constructing history, consider publishing the result in some way. School boards, alumni associations, or parent-teacher associations may be willing to publish a good history of their institutions. Local foundations are often interested in publishing information on local education. The more active historical societies publish journals or newsletters and are often eager to consider well-written essays. The very best article-length essays may gain a place in a good state or regional historical journal, while essays written in a more popular or journalistic style may be candidates for the local paper or a regional magazine.

While you should remain open to the possibility of publishing your history in a book, booklet, or article, that is not the only avenue open to you. Consider an exhibit at a college or school or at a local historical society. Such an exhibit will display the photographs, artifacts, and perhaps excerpts from oral history interviews. Extensive captions, a brochure, or a written guide to the exhibit can provide the public with your explanation of the material and your interpretation of the history you are presenting.

What about a slide-tape presentation? Video cassette recorders are now

Exhibiting the History of Nearby Education

When the Dade County, Florida, Public Schools celebrated their centennial in 1985, they pulled out all the stops. Dade County recounted its school history through classroom activities, a museum exhibit, an attractively designed booklet, a festival showcasing the finest student talent in art, music, drama, and dance, a banquet for leading educators and businesspeople, and even a float for the educational system. Asterie Baker Provenzo and Eugene F. Provenzo, Jr., are now at work on a full length history of the schools.

Such a range of activities required a high level of financial support from the local business community. Nonetheless, the Dade County celebration suggests the variety of ways one can reach the public with the history of local education on even a modest budget. The Provenzos's experience with the museum exhibit provides an example of an innovative means of presenting your history. Schools, businesses, and libraries, as well as local historical museums, are likely sites for a well-conceived exhibit.

"School Days—A Class Act for 100 Years," an exhibit that examined the complex mission of the Dade County Public Schools and celebrated the system's accomplishments over the past 100 years, occupied 1,800 square feet of space at the Historical Museum of Southern Florida in early 1986. We guest-curated the exhibit, which was partially financed by corporate donations and designed and mounted by the museum staff.

The multidimensional exhibit was made up of four major components. Visitors entered through a hallway, chock-full of artifacts and memorabilia such as lockers, plaques, kindergarten chairs, trophies, school letters, and athletic equipment. A time-line history of the school system, divided into decades, included a narrative text, photographs, the first school board minutes, textbooks, and documents as diverse as ledger books from the 1890s and a letter from the superintendent during the 1930s admonishing teachers not to wear lipstick. Newspaper clippings, official school system publications, report cards, prom and commencement memorabilia, and examples of student work were also displayed. The third component of the exhibit profiled four schools, chosen because they were the first high school (white), the first black high school, a consolidated school, which at one time was the largest in the nation, and the first modern-day bilingual elementary school. This element of the exhibit included uniforms, photographs, documents, plaques, student

At the exhibit's entry, a large black and white photo of an early Miami High School study hall provided a backdrop for the exhibit's introductory text.

Visitors passed through this memorabilia hall, with photographs, textbooks, and other artifacts from the schools arranged by decade. Beyond this point lay exhibits profiling four Dade County schools and a model classroom.

work, and other memorabilia. The exhibition also included a recon-
structed classroom, furnished to represent a typical late 1950s to early
1960s elementary school classroom in Dade County. Classes of visit-
ing schoolchildren used the classroom, pursuing lessons on issues from
the period such as civil defense drills, segregated education, and the
space race.

The mounting of the exhibit and the publicity about the museum's
efforts brought responses from the school system, individual schools,
and former teachers and students in the community that made possi-
ble the collection of photographs, documents, and artifacts that reflect
the history of the system. Many of these artifacts were donated to the
museum, where they will be kept and made available to those interested
in doing historical research on the schools. Not only did the exhibit pro-
vide the general public the opportunity to learn about the history of the
school system, to indulge in a little nostalgia, and to reflect upon the
complexity of the mission of the Dade County Public Schools, but it also
acted as the catalyst for the location, collection, and preservation of a
tremendous amount of documentation on the history of the system at
both the individual school level and the institutional level.

Asterie Baker Provenzo and Eugene F. Provenzo, Jr., prepared this
selection especially for this volume. Asterie Baker Provenzo is a free-
lance writer and historian. Eugene F. Provenzo, Jr., is a professor at
the School of Education and Allied Professions, University of Miami.

The late 'fifties era classroom was used by the museum's teachers to instruct students in the museum's fourth grade program.

nearly as common as televisions sets—might a video presentation be effective? Either option would allow effective use of photographs and other material culture items. An audio-tape presentation is another option, one that could be used in conjunction with some of your better reproductions from oral history interviews. Or script a dramatization for presentation before the local historical society or on campus. Any of these ideas may be integrated into the sort of exhibit mentioned above, as well. Some creative thought may suggest other means of bringing your history to the community.

No matter what medium you decide upon, you will need to do at least some writing, probably quite a bit. Don't flinch from that task. It is seldom easy. *But don't avoid it.* We frequently think we know a thing, but when we are forced to state it formally, we find we do not know it as well as we thought. Writing forces us to be precise, logical, and clear. We may discover that our ideas were imprecise, confused, and awkward. Writing about what we have constructed, then, helps us locate problems with the structure. It also teaches us to think better.

So write. Do not wait until all the evidence is in file boxes before beginning to write, either. As various aspects of the project begin to take shape, as certain questions begin to find their answers, write a few lines, a paragraph, a page or more to explain to yourself what you are perceiving.

Finally, ask the librarian at the local historical society or at the public library if those organizations are interested in obtaining a copy of whatever product you have constructed. Ask, too, if the library has an interest in adding to its resources your oral history tapes, private photographs you have taken or collected, and any other resources that might have come into your possession in the course of your work.

If you have come this far, trying the suggestions made here, you have doubtlessly gained some new skills and a number of new insights. Don't stop now. Extend your skills. Broaden your reseach horizon. There are whole forgotten worlds of a nearby past for you to recover.

Suggested Readings

There are a number of books available on historical methodology, some of which I have already cited in earlier chapters. Anyone doing serious research in history should take time to read one or two thoughtfully. In addition to Barzun and Gaff, Winks, Davidson and Lytle, and Bloch, this discussion of the evaluation of evidence drew from Robert Jones Shafer, ed., *A Guide to Historical Method*, rev. ed. (Homewood, Ill.: Dorsey Press, 1974)—the quotation is from page 159—and was influenced by David Hackett Fischer, *Historians' Falla-*

cies: Toward a Logic of Historical Thought (New York: Harper & Row, 1970); and J.H. Hexter, *The History Primer* (New York: Basic Books, 1971).

Several of the sources cited in chapters 4 and 5 include important cautions about the biases inherent in various types of evidence. See also Lydia Lucas, "The Historian in the Archives: Limitations of Primary Source Materials," *Minnesota History* 47 (Summer 1981): 227-32; and David J. Meltzer, "Ideology and Material Culture," in *Modern Material Culture: The Archeology of Us,* edited by Richard A. Gould and Michael B. Schiffer (New York: Academic Press, 1981), pp. 113-26. John H. Ralph, "Bias in Historical School Enrollment Figures," *Historical Methods* 12 (Fall 1980): 215-21, is highly statistical and difficult but worth reading by those who intend to do higher level quantitative work with enrollment data. Research using photographs extensively would benefit from James Borchert, "Historical Photo-Analysis: A Research Method," *Historical Methods* 15 (Spring 1982): 35-44.

Both Thomas E. Felt, *Researching, Writing, and Publishing Local History* (Nashville: American Association for State and Local History, 1976) and David E. Kyvig and Myron A. Marty, *Nearby History: Exploring the Past around You* (Nashville: American Association for State and Local History, 1982) have wise words about writing and publishing nearby history.

The Nearby History of Education:
A Brief Bibliographical Essay

I HAVE TWO OBJECTIVES IN THIS ESSAY. THE FIRST is to provide a guide to some of the better general literature in the history of education in the United States. As I have maintained throughout the volume, it is essential to gain a strong sense of historical developments in education generally before constructing a history of education in a specific locality. The larger context in which education developed is crucial to understanding the continuities and changes in a community's schools. This discussion of general sources is not comprehensive; rather it is intended to introduce some particularly valuable and provocative studies. There are hundreds of other worthy books and articles beyond those noted here, and a researcher will want to sample many of them.

My second objective is to indicate many of the professional books and articles based on local history. Professional historians frequently use a nearby focus. By studying an issue in one locality, the historian is able to investigate it intensively, using the community as a case study. If similar patterns in a number of localities are found, the historian can begin to generalize about the patterns.

Professional studies of nearby education can serve as models of the kinds of research that can be done, the sorts of documents that others have found, and questions that can be investigated. My intention in this essay is to introduce some of the best of this growing literature.

One should start with a broad national study of educational history. Recent work in the national context includes Joel Spring, *The American School, 1649-1985* (New York: Longman, 1985); Robert L. Church and Michael W. Sedlak, *Education in the United States: An Interpretive History* (New York: Free Press, 1976); and the projected three volume study by Lawrence A. Cremin, two volumes of which are now available: *American Education: The*

Colonial Experience, 1607-1783 (New York: Harper and Row, 1970); and *American Education: The National Experience, 1783-1876* (New York: Harper and Row, 1980). Samuel Bowles and Herbert Gintis, in *Schooling in Capitalist America* (New York: Basic Books, 1976), raise a number of provocative issues that have caused historians to investigate new questions. My students like David Nasaw's *Schooled to Order: A Social History of Public Schooling in the United States* (New York: Oxford University Press, 1976). Andrew Gulliford's *America's Country Schools* (Washington, D.C.: Preservation Press, 1984) is a richly illustrated introduction to rural schooling, while David B. Tyack's *The One Best System: A History of American Urban Education* (Cambridge, Mass.: Harvard University Press, 1974) provides a good starting point for studies of urban schooling.

Chronologically and topically more tightly focused studies of public schools include Carl F. Kaestle, *Pillars of the Republic: Common Schools and American Society, 1780-1860* (New York: Hill and Wang, 1983); Joel Spring, *Education and the Rise of the Corporate State* (Boston: Beacon Press, 1972); and Lawrence A. Cremin, *The Transformation of the School: Progressivism in American Education, 1876-1957* (New York: Vintage Books, 1964). The recent past is dealt with in sharply contrasting approaches by Diane Ravitch, *The Troubled Crusade: American Education, 1945-1980* (New York: Basic Books, 1983); and Ira Shor, *Culture Wars: School and Society in the Conservative Restoration, 1969-1984* (Boston: Routledge & Kegan Paul, 1986).

The history of higher education has received a good deal of attention from historians. The standard introduction to the history of higher education is Frederick Rudolph, *The American College and University: A History* (New York: Vintage Books, 1962). Laurence R. Veysey's *The Emergence of the American University* (Chicago: University of Chicago Press, 1965) focuses on higher education's pivotal half-century after the Civil War. Frederick Rudolph's *Curriculum: A History of the American Undergraduate Course of Study since 1636* (San Francisco: Jossey-Bass Publishers, 1977) provides a good introduction to the changing content of college education, while problems of the freedom of teachers to shape curriculum and research are explored in Richard Hofstadter and Walter P. Metzger's *The Development of Academic Freedom in the United States* (New York: Columbia University Press, 1955). David F. Allmendinger investigates college innovations and student life in *Paupers and Scholars: The Transformation of Student Life in Nineteenth-Century New England* (New York: St. Martin's Press, 1975).

From the Colonial period through much of the nineteenth century, secondary education took place in academies. Theodore R. Sizer, ed., *The Age of the Academies* (New York: Teachers College, Columbia University, 1964) provides a brief introduction to these ubiquitous, diverse institutions. Elite boarding schools, distinct from the academies in many ways, began to emerge in mid-century, along with the public high school. James McLachlan, *American Boarding Schools: A Historical Study* (New York: Charles Scribner's Sons, 1970) investigates the former, while the latter are studied in Edward A. Krug, *The Shaping of the American High School, 1880-1920* (Madison: University of Wisconsin Press, 1964); and Krug's *The Shaping of the American High School, 1920-1941* (Madison: University of Wisconsin Press, 1972). Any work on secondary education should be supplemented with Joseph F. Kett's *Rites of Passage: Adolescence in America, 1790 to the Present* (New York: Basic Books, 1977).

Teachers and administrators still await thorough historical investigation, though administrators and the forms of school administration have received more attention than teachers. Paul Mattingly, *The Classless Profession: American Schoolmen in the Nineteenth Century* (New York: New York University Press, 1975) is a good starting place for the history of teachers. Raymond Callahan, *Education and the Cult of Efficiency* (Chicago: University of Chicago Press, 1962), and David B. Tyack and Elisabeth Hansot, *Managers of Virtue: Public School Leadership in America, 1820-1980* (New York: Basic Books, 1982) provide important insights into educational administration.

Meyer Weinberg, *A Chance to Learn: A History of Race and Education in the United States* (Cambridge, Eng.: Cambridge University Press, 1977) surveys minority education generally. The essays in Vincent P. Franklin and James D. Anderson, eds., *New Perspectives on Black Educational History* (Boston: G.K. Hall & Co., 1978) deal with Afro-American schooling more specifically, while the standard source for black schooling in the American South is Henry Allen Bullock, *A History of Negro Education in the South, from 1619 to the Present* (New York: Praeger, 1967). There is no general source for women's education yet, but much can be gained from Barbara Miller Solomon, *In the Company of Educated Women: A History of Women and Higher Education in America* (New Haven: Yale University Press, 1985); and Barbara M. Cross, *The Educated Woman in America* (New York: Teachers College, Columbia University, 1965).

One should gain as much information as possible on state-level developments in education. Nearly every state has at least one general history of its schools, such as David Murray, *History of Education in New Jersey* (Washington D.C.: Government Printing Office, 1899); and George H. Martin, *The Evolution of the Massachusetts Public School System* (New York: D. Appleton and Company, 1904). Most of these sources should be read skeptically, however. Many are badly dated, and it is probably safe to say that most are uncritically laudatory.

For more general information on the history of education in the United States, see Francesco Cordasco and William Brickman, eds., *A Bibliography of American Educational History: An Annotated and Classified Guide* (New York: AMS Press, 1975), and Jurgen Herbst, *The History of American Education* (Northbrook, Ill.: AHM Publishing Corp., 1973).

The remainder of this essay will introduce examples of histories of education that use a nearby focus. These, too, of course, provide that necessary sense of context. For our purposes, they also provide models of the type of historical work described in this volume.

We now have excellent general histories of education in particular cities. Among the best recent offerings are Selwyn K. Troen, *The Public and the Schools: Shaping the St. Louis System, 1838-1920* (Columbia: University of Missouri Press, 1975); Carl F. Kaestle, *The Evolution of an Urban School System: New York City, 1750-1850* (Cambridge, Mass.: Harvard University Press, 1973); and Stanley K. Schultz, *The Culture Factory: Boston Public Schools, 1789-1860* (New York: Oxford University Press, 1973). Tina H. Sheller, "The Origins of Public Education in Baltimore, 1825-1829," *History of Education Quarterly* 22 (Spring 1982): 23-44, provides evidence from a brief period of time to compare with the origins of urban education elsewhere. Among other good general studies of education in a single city, see Charles D. Biebel, "Cultural Change on the Southwest Frontier: Albuquerque Schooling, 1870-1895," *New Mexico Historical Quarterly* 55 (July 1980): 209-30.

Histories of individual institutions are legion. Colleges, especially, are the subject of truckloads of studies. From them we can learn more than many of us care to know about college presidents and politics. They are less helpful if we are interested in curricular development, philosophies of learning, struggles for academic freedom, student life, and opportunities for the poor, women, or minorities. See for example, Suzanne Rau Wolfe, *The University of Alabama* (University: University of Alabama Press, 1983); or Russell E. Miller, *Light on the Hill: A History of Tufts College, 1852-1952* (Boston: Beacon Press, 1966). Much stronger traditional institutional studies include Thomas Dyer, *The University of Georgia: A Bicentennial History, 1785-1985* (Athens: University of Georgia Press, 1985); E. Wilson Lyon, *The History of Pomona College, 1887-1969* (Claremont, Calif.: Pomona College, 1977); and Frederick S. Allen, and others, *The University of Colorado, 1876-1976* (New York: Harcourt Brace Jovanovich, 1976). Among the few that include good material on students is Merle E. Curti and Vernon R. Carstensen, *The University of Wisconsin: A History, 1848-1925* (Madison: University of Wisconsin Press, 1949).

Many institutional studies suffer from a lack of sensitivity to historical developments beyond the walls of the institution. Among studies that do particularly good jobs of connecting their stories with contemporary events in society and culture, see David C. Humphrey, *From King's College to Columbia, 1746-1800* (New York: Columbia University Press, 1976); and Jane G. Rushing and Kline A. Nall, *Evolution of a University: Texas Tech's First Fifty Years* (Austin, Tex.: Madrona Press, 1975).

Newer studies of individual institutions that have broken new ground in terms of methodology and issues include Jane Sanders, *Cold War on Campus: Academic Freedom at the University of Washington, 1946-1964* (Seattle: University of Washington Press, 1979); James Summerville, *Educating Black Doctors: A History of Meharry Medical College* (University: University of Alabama Press, 1983); and most notably Martin Duberman, *Black Mountain: An Exploration in Community* (Garden City, N.Y.: Anchor Press / Doubleday, 1972). James D. Anderson, "Northern Philanthropy and the Training of Black Leadership: Fisk University, a Case Study, 1915-1930," in Franklin and Anderson, eds., *New Perspectives on Black Educational History*, pp. 61-96, illustrates the insights available using a single institution to explore an issue.

The biographies of institutions may usefully explore issues beyond the specific institutions in question. Two recent articles, for example, effectively trace turn-of-the-century child welfare programs through studies of single schools. See Priscilla Ferguson Clement, "With Wise and Benevolent Purpose: Poor Children and the State Public School at Owatonna, 1885-1915," *Minnesota History* 49 (Spring 1984): 2-13; and R.S. Patterson and Patricia Rooke, "The Delicate Duty of Child Saving: Coldwater, Michigan, 1876-1896," *Michigan History* 61 (Fall 1977): 194-219. We can learn a great deal about curricular innovations that affected schools throughout the country by investigating the ideas and forces at work in innovations at the local level, as Bayly Ellen Marks does in "Liberal Education in the Gilded Age: Baltimore and the Creation of the Manual Training School," *Maryland Historical Magazine* 74 (September 1979): 238-52. This essay also furnishes, incidentally, a splendid example of a researcher who paid very careful attention to the broader intellectual currents. In a masterful essay, Wayne Fuller uses the history of a particular rural school district to explore the concept of community; see "School District 37: Prairie Community," *Western Historical Quarterly* 12 (October 1981): 419-32.

Historians of the black educational experience have been particularly adept at using the local case study as a means of illuminating issues in minority education. Whether one's interest is in minority education or not, Vincent P. Franklin, *The Education of Black Philadelphia: The Social and Educational History of a Minority Community, 1900-1950* (Philadelphia: University of Pennsylvania Press, 1979) should top the reading list of historians of nearby education. Michael W. Homel, *Down from Equality: Black Chicagoans and the Public Schools, 1920-41* (Chicago: University of Chicago Press, 1984) is a model of tightly focused, carefully argued nearby history. Among other researchers in minority education who use a nearby focus effectively, see June O. Patton, "The Black Community of Augusta and the Struggle for Ware High School, 1880-1899," in Franklin and Anderson, eds., *New Perspectives on Black Educational History*, pp. 45-60.

Other ethnic and minority groups have likewise been the subjects of solid research based on nearby records. Chicago's Catholic population received its due in James W. Sanders, *The Education of Urban Minorities: Catholics in Chicago, 1833-1965* (New York: Oxford University Press, 1977). Maxine Seller has written several essays on immigrants in Buffalo, including "The Education of Immigrant Children in Buffalo, New York, 1890-1916," *New York History* 57 (April 1976): 183-99.

Women's education has received increasing attention from historians in the last decade, and some telling work has used the local case study approach. See for example Sandra P. Epstein, "Women and Legal Education: The Case of Boalt Hall," *Pacific Historian* 28 (Fall 1984): 5-22; Charlotte Williams Conable, *Women at Cornell: The Myth of Equal Education* (Ithaca, N.Y.: Cornell University Press, 1977); and Anne Firor Scott's fascinating research in a single institution's archives, in "The Ever Widening Circle: The Diffusion of Feminist Values from the Troy Female Seminary, 1822-1872," *History of Education Quarterly* 19 (Spring 1979): 3-25.

Some historians have used nearby history to illuminate specific issues in the development of education. Paul McBride focused on Beverly, Massachusetts, to probe the ideology and reality of early vocational training; see "The Co-Op Industrial Education Movement," *History of Education Quarterly* 14 (Summer 1974): 209-22. Sol Cohen, *The Progressives and Urban School*

Reform (New York: Teachers College, Columbia University, 1964); and Julia Wrigley, *Class, Politics and Public Schools: Chicago 1900-1950* (New Brunswick, N.J.: Rutgers University Press, 1982) deal with school reform efforts in the first half of the century in New York and Chicago, respectively. Compulsory attendance, the bane of every bored schoolchild, was studied in Richard Ives, "Compulsory Education and the St. Louis Public School System, 1905-1907," *Missouri Historical Review* 71 (April 1977): 315-29. Jeffrey Mirel used Detroit as a case study in the problem of education in times of economic reversal in "The Politics of Educational Retrenchment in Detroit, 1929-1935," *History of Education Quarterly* 24 (Fall 1984): 323-59; while Gary L. Peltier used Denver to study "Teacher Participation in Curriculum Revision: An Historical Case Study," *History of Education Quarterly* 7 (Summer 1967): 209-19. Similarly, efforts of socialist working people to affect the education of working-class children have been explored by William J. Reese in his prize-winning "'Partisans of the Proletariat': The Socialist Working Class and the Milwaukee Schools, 1890-1920," *History of Education Quarterly* 21 (Spring 1981): 3-50. Michael B. Katz has had a profound effect on history of education; he is tightly wedded to the case study approach. Among many other essays, see his "The 'New Departure' in Quincy, 1873-1881: The Nature of Nineteenth Century Educational Reform," *New England Quarterly* 40 (March 1967): 3-30.

Teachers as a group have not been studied as closely as they deserve, but what little we have is often based on local studies. See, for instance, William H. Issel, "Teachers and Educational Reform during the Progressive Era: A Case Study of the Pittsburgh Teachers Association," *History of Education Quarterly* 7 (Summer 1967): 220-33; or my "Frontier Teacher: Arizona, 1875-1925," *Journal of the West* 16 (July 1977): 54-66, which draws its data from a county-level investigation. Richard B. Fishbane uses census records and other seldom-used sources effectively in "'The Shallow Boast of Cheapness': Public School Teaching as a Profession in Philadelphia, 1865-1890," *Pennsylvania Magazine of History and Biography* 103 (January 1979): 66-84.

Students and student life likewise deserve much more study, and nearby education is already proving to be a fertile source. David F. Allmendinger, Jr., "Mount Holyoke Students Encounter the Need for Life Planning, 1837-1850," *History of Education Quarterly* 19 (Spring 1979): 27-46, provides a glimpse into the changing patterns of young women's lives in the nineteenth century. Sarah Gordon, "Smith College Students: The First Ten Classes, 1879-1888," *History of Education Quarterly* 15 (Summer 1975): 147-68, uses student records to reconstruct student life; while Cynthia Horsburgh Requardt, "Alternative Professions for Goucher College Graduates, 1892-1910," *Maryland Historical Magazine* 74 (September 1979): 274-81, uses alumnae records to see what roles educated women were taking on near the turn of the century.

Running through much of this literature, as through much of the work in social history generally, is the question of the distribution of social, economic, and political power, and hence, ultimately the question of social class. Many of the essays noted above deal directly or indirectly with the relationship of schooling to one's position in society. The effect of social class on school achievement at the turn of the century has recently been explored using a local case study; see Joel Perlmann, "Who Stayed in School? Social Structure and Academic Achievement in the Determination of Enrollment Patterns, Providence, Rhode Island, 1880-1925," *Journal of American History* 72 (December 1985): 588-614. The use of education in class consolidation is explored by Ronald Story, "Harvard and the Boston Brahmins: A Study in Institutional and Class Development, 1800-1865," *Journal of Social History* 8 (Spring 1975): 94-121; and Alan Creutz, "Social Access to the Professions: Late Nineteenth-Century Academics at the University of Michigan as a Case Study," *Journal of Social History* 15 (Fall 1981): 73-87. Joel Perlmann, "Working-Class Homeownership and Children's Schooling in Providence, Rhode Island, 1880-1925," *History of Education Quarterly* 23 (Summer 1983): 175-94; and Reed Ueda, "The High School and Social Mobility in a Streetcar Suburb: Somerville, Massachusetts, 1870-1910," *Journal of Interdisciplinary History* 14 (Spring 1984): 751-71, are more concerned with the other end of the hierarchy and its relationship to schooling.

This essay by no means exhausts the sorts of topics that historians are pursuing through local history of education, nor the range of essays and books that have been written using a nearby focus. But it does indicate a few of the better sources one can read to gain insights, ideas for sources, and points of departure. Read broadly as you research deeply.

Index